LINCOLN CENTER

LINCOLN CENTER

A PROMISE REALIZED, 1979–2006

Stephen Stamas
Sharon Zane

LINCOLN CENTER for the Performing Arts

BICENTENNIAL 1807 WILEY 2007 BICENTENNIAL

John Wiley & Sons, Inc.

This book is printed on acid-free paper. ♾

Published by John Wiley & Sons, Inc., Hoboken, New Jersey
Published simultaneously in Canada

Library of Congress Cataloging-in-Publication Data:

Stamas, Stephen.
Lincoln Center : a promise realized, 1979-2006 / Stephen Stamas and Sharon Zane.
p. cm.
Includes bibliographical references and index.
ISBN-13: 978-0-470-10123-0 (cloth)
ISBN-10: 0-470-10123-7 (cloth)
1. Lincoln Center for the Performing Arts. 2. Performing arts—New York (State)—New York—History—20th century. 3. Performing arts—New York (State)—New York—History—21st century. I. Zane, Sharon. II. Title.
PN1588.N5S73 2006
790.209747'1—dc22

2006029948

Printed in the United States of America

10 9 8 7 6 5 4 3 2 1

CONTENTS

PREFACE

The partnership between Lincoln Center for the Performing Arts—the umbrella entity created in the late 1950s to serve as the organizing framework and the real-estate manager of the arts center at Broadway and 65th Street—and its constituent resident artistic companies is surely one of the great success stories of our time. Yet inherent in that relationship have been tensions that occasionally have led to differences between the Center and its resident organizations, also known as constituents. How much power and influence does each have in relation to the other? How are funds raised and distributed? What constitutes programming competition among the various players? Despite these issues, Lincoln Center itself, including the programming it sponsors, and its resident organizations have prospered and produced a half century of excellence in their offerings and global leadership in the field of the performing arts.

This is not a chronicle per se of Lincoln Center's separate resident artistic companies. Each of them—the Chamber Music Society of Lincoln Center; the Film Society of Lincoln Center; Jazz at Lincoln Center; the Juilliard School; Lincoln Center for the Performing Arts,

Inc.; Lincoln Center Theater; the Metropolitan Opera; the New York City Ballet; the New York City Opera; the New York Philharmonic; the New York Public Library for the Performing Arts; and the School of American Ballet—has its own management and board and is financially and artistically autonomous, even as it functions as part of the Lincoln Center "family." Rather, this history is an account of how the umbrella organization known as Lincoln Center for the Performing Arts has evolved to serve and support the "family" in their own remarkable artistic achievements while at the same time broadening the program offerings at the Center to attract a wider public. In the main, this history seeks to accomplish this by telling a series of stories about the major milestones of the last two and a half decades that together comprise the artistic, physical, and administrative history of Lincoln Center. It also acknowledges the complicated relationship between the Center and its constituents as they have worked together in pursuit of Lincoln Center's overall primary purpose: the presentation of excellence in the performing arts. This chronicle does touch upon the histories of specific constituents insofar as Lincoln Center played a central role in their creation—as with Jazz at Lincoln Center, the Chamber Music Society of Lincoln Center, and the Film Society of Lincoln Center—or where the Center provided substantial support during difficult times, as with the Lincoln Center Theater.

What follows in this history is intended as an updating of Edgar B. Young's 1980 book *Lincoln Center: The Building of an Institution*. Young, who played an important part in the establishment of Lincoln Center as a representative of John D. Rockefeller 3rd, has already documented much of the period from 1955 to 1980. With Mr. Young's encouragement, we have included in this account a fuller discussion of some of the developments in the 1970s that help to carry the story forward through June 2006, the end point of the current history.

In the twenty-seven preceding years, Lincoln Center moved well beyond its considerable administrative and real-estate responsibilities to become a major force in programming in areas not covered by its resident organizations, a role contemplated for it from the beginning. This impetus to fill artistic programming gaps had been reflected in the initiatives of the late William Schuman, the president of Lincoln Center in the 1960s, but financial difficulties and the concerns of the constituents about fund-raising and possible program competition put an end to some of his efforts. With growing financial strength and a clearer purpose, which ameliorated the concerns of the resident organizations, Lincoln Center realized in the period of this history much of Schuman's initial vision and contributed further to the luster of what the world at large refers to as "Lincoln Center." Yet it is important to keep in mind that central to the institution's luster is the artistic brilliance of its constituents and their achievements over the years.

In the end, this is the story of how Lincoln Center for the Performing Arts has served and supported its constituent groups while producing its own innovative artistic programming and how, in the process, it became a role model for other performing arts organizations around the world.

ACKNOWLEDGMENTS

Special thanks are due to the Lincoln Center Directors Emeriti Council, cochaired by June Noble Larkin and Martin E. Segal, for initiating this project to update the history of Lincoln Center. Grants from the Directors Emeriti Council, as well as additional financial support from Lincoln Center, made this project possible.

In addition, the Lincoln Center staff has been patient and helpful to us as we researched the files, the oral histories, and other records that serve as the basis for this history. Judith Johnson, the archivist at Lincoln Center, and her associates made special efforts in assisting with searches and preparing a chronology of major events, a version of which is included in our text. The Lincoln Center Archives are a remarkable asset.

We also thank Susan DeMark for her resourceful research assistance. It was a pleasure to work with her. In addition, we thank Peter Johnson for his helpful editorial suggestions and Martin Timins for his expert initial copyediting.

Finally, we are grateful to Bonnie Zitofsky for keeping track of us and coordinating our many fruitful meetings.

We have found our own collaboration an easy and rewarding one. While the writing of different sections was divided between us, the final product is the result of joint consultation and discussion and reflects our joint judgments and conclusions.

Stephen Stamas
Sharon Zane

INTRODUCTION

IN THE SPRING OF 1979, AS LINCOLN CENTER PREPARED TO celebrate the twentieth anniversary of its ground breaking, there was much for which to be grateful. In many respects, the dream of its founder, John D. Rockefeller 3rd, that a center be established to be used "for the advancement of the arts and for the benefit of the people who come to attend its performances,"[1] had been realized. He, along with his associates, had envisioned a place "built not just for today or tomorrow, but for generations to come," where "the arts are not for the privileged few, but for the many. Their place is not on the periphery of daily life, but at its center. They should function not merely as another form of entertainment but, rather, should contribute significantly to our well-being and happiness."[2]

A spectacular, free-to-the-public outdoor sound and light show mounted for the occasion, showcasing many of the performance highlights of the Center's first twenty years, drew crowds to the plaza throughout the summer of 1979. At the time, Center president John Mazzola told the press, "New York is the cultural capital of the world, and this celebration underlines that in gold."[3]

Much had been accomplished in the twenty years following the 1959 groundbreaking ceremony. The centerpiece of a massive federally funded urban renewal effort for the Upper West Side, Lincoln Center could measure its success in a number of ways. It had sparked an economic renaissance that changed the face of that once blighted neighborhood; restaurants, chic shops, and new upscale residential towers sprang up around the Center, stimulating similar development northward just as the urban planners had anticipated. As a result, the City of New York enjoyed substantially increased real-estate tax revenues from the area.[4] Fifty million ticket buyers had attended some thirty-one thousand performances in the seventeen years since First Lady Jacqueline Kennedy attended the Center's televised opening performance in 1962 at Philharmonic Hall, generating a substantial increase in pedestrian and vehicular traffic.[5]

Lincoln Center's sixteen-acre campus, with imposing buildings by seven of the world's leading architects and peaceful outdoor public spaces designed by one of the country's leading landscape architects, offered visitors every opportunity to congregate, to sit in peaceful surroundings, or to enjoy exciting outdoor programming. Its plazas and open spaces beckoned, and New Yorkers and visitors from near and far took great advantage of them.

As the nation's first performing arts complex, Lincoln Center had already served as the model for a growing number of similar enterprises, both in the United States and abroad. Yet, according to the *New York Times*, no other center had been able to match the

Aerial view of the original Lincoln Center campus as it appeared in 1979, its twentieth anniversary. Proceeding around the Josie Robertson Plaza from the left: the New York State Theater, the Metropolitan Opera House, and Avery Fisher Hall. To the right of the opera house, the Vivian Beaumont Theater and the New York Public Library for the Performing Arts. To the right of Avery Fisher Hall, the Juilliard School.

richness of the artistic concentration at Lincoln Center.[6] Much more than the sum of its parts, Lincoln Center's dynamic artistic life was everywhere apparent. Already an unofficial New York City landmark, Lincoln Center had become a destination not only for eager audiences enjoying the many and varied pleasures within but also for multitudes of tourists from all over the world.

The Center, as originally contemplated, was physically complete by 1979. Philharmonic Hall, with its problematic acoustics, had been completely renovated and renamed to honor its major donor, Avery Fisher. The Chamber Music Society of Lincoln Center and the Film Society of Lincoln Center had been added to its list of resident organizations. And the Lincoln Center Institute for the Arts in Education, the Center's pioneering effort in aesthetic education, had been established, broadening and deepening the scope of its commitment to Rockefeller's original vision that Lincoln Center would not only preserve the past but also nourish the future. *Live from Lincoln Center*, broadcast to millions of appreciative viewers and showcasing many memorable performances by participating constituents, had extended the Center's reach beyond anyone's wildest dream. Lincoln Center was, in the words of President Carter, "a magnet for artists and lovers of the arts everywhere."[7]

Yet amid these singular accomplishments, troublesome challenges remained—challenges that even Lincoln Center's most ardent admirers could not ignore. For one thing, in 1979, the Center's finances were in a precarious state. Operating and maintenance costs had continued to climb. With its halls running deficits that were only deepened by high inflation and New York City's unprecedented fiscal crisis in the mid-1970s, the issues of communal fund-raising and fund-apportionment affected relations with the constituent organizations. Some critics pointed to continuing acoustical problems in Avery Fisher Hall and the New York State Theater. The Vivian Beaumont Theater, once the Center's showplace for drama, had been dark for two years, a constituent in name only.

Artist Larry Rivers's model of Lincoln Center, decorated with icing and flowers, constructed for the List Print and Poster Program poster that was issued in 1979 to celebrate Lincoln Center's twentieth anniversary.

According to some people, the first twenty years had not resulted in enough of the kind of collaboration and cross-fertilization among the constituents that Rockefeller and his associates had hoped for. Pressed for operating funds and the need to develop and retain audiences, the constituents were seen as jealously guarding their own territories and thus depriving the Center of a true sense of community. One critic even referred to it as a "shopping center for the arts" that has "yet to come to grips with integrating."[8]

Perhaps most troubling at the moment of its twentieth anniversary was the feeling that Lincoln Center had yet to define its true purpose, beyond that of real-estate manager. From the start, the founders had recognized that offerings in addition to those the resident constituents presented would be required if Lincoln Center were to truly represent all the performing arts, although, Richard Shepard of the *New York Times* reported, "how much of Lincoln Center's central function would be more than administrative was not spelled out."[9]

The additional role of Lincoln Center as a producer had begun to emerge as early as the mid-1960s. The need to fill the halls year-round was a potent catalyst. So, too, was the recognition that the Center's offerings should appeal to as broad a public as possible. Several programming initiatives, including the establishment of its long-lived Mostly Mozart and Great Performers series, extended the performing-arts season and filled in gaps in the programming of the resident companies. The groundbreaking initiative of *Live from Lincoln Center* brought international notice to the participating constituents and the Center itself. As Shepard pointed out, though, "whatever feeling there is that Lincoln Center should be a setting for artistic mingling that would step over the bounds of organization is counterbalanced by a desire for non-interference."[10] In this environment, critics called for more innovative programming on the part of the Center and its constituents, vital leadership, better fund-raising, and more audience-friendly facilities. If, from the very start, the role of Lincoln Center in relation to its resident companies was never clear, this appeared to be ever more the case at the moment of its twentieth anniversary.

Much has been accomplished in many areas since 1979. In its role of real-estate manager, Lincoln Center spearheaded one major building project—the Samuel B. and David Rose Building—and recently has embarked upon another, the ten-year redevelopment project that will transform much of the campus by 2010. In providing programming, Lincoln Center for the Performing Arts, Inc., has transcended its early role as occasional producer. Its impact as an organizing entity that produces a wide range of successful programming and educational initiatives has extended the founders' initial vision that the Center itself would "encourage, sponsor or facilitate performances or exhibitions, commission the creation of works of musical and performing art, and voluntarily assist the education of artists or students of the arts."[11] Yet, in the end, it is the strength of its constituents—who were at the heart of the Lincoln Center enterprise from the very start—that truly defines the Center and makes it the important cultural force it is today.

Now, forty-seven years after President Dwight David Eisenhower, sterling-silver shovel ceremonially in hand, broke ground on behalf of Lincoln Center's trustees, constituents, and future patrons on May 14, 1959, to signal the beginning of the vast construction project, Lincoln Center is on solid financial footing. The Center is able to support its constituents in myriad ways that contribute to their financial stability and thus to their continuing artistic vitality. The revival of Lincoln Center Theater, now with a two-decade string of critical and commercial successes behind it, and the establishment of Jazz at Lincoln Center, would not have been possible without the financial support of Lincoln Center. Its halls are rented year-round and do not present a financial burden to the constituents. Exciting new programming breathes life into the efforts of Lincoln Center, Inc., to draw younger audiences. The Lincoln Center Institute's innovative programs have been copied by similar entities throughout the country.

Able staff and volunteer leadership have permitted Lincoln Center to successfully meet the many challenges it has faced over the last twenty-plus years. Today, an aging campus, aging audiences, and an unpredictable economic scene present a new set of challenges. Lincoln Center's redevelopment project—which will redesign, renovate, and renew the Center's public spaces, buildings, and halls—addresses the first of these challenges. To appeal to new and younger audiences, keeping in mind the changing demographics of the city and the nation, the Center will need to further extend and enrich its programming. It must identify sources of financial support among sectors of the business community that are new to the performing arts. Finally, Lincoln Center must ensure that the name Lincoln Center for the Performing Arts, and all that it stands for, remains squarely front and center in the public's eye. The strength of the institution, its leadership, and its mission will be important assets in meeting these challenges.

1

ALL IN THE FAMILY
Lincoln Center and Its Constituents

LINCOLN CENTER, INC., HAS SUCCESSFULLY NURTURED AND encouraged the creation of three independent constituents—the Chamber Music Society of Lincoln Center, the Film Society of Lincoln Center, and Jazz at Lincoln Center—and welcomed a fourth, the School of American Ballet, as self-sustaining organizations with their own boards and operating budgets. In addition, its management helped to rescue the Lincoln Center Theater Company and dealt with the unfortunate demise of another, Music Theater at Lincoln Center.

Music Theater at Lincoln Center

When the New York State Theater opened its doors in the spring of 1964, it had only one official tenant, the Music Theater of Lincoln Center. Negotiations with City Center on the terms for incorporating the New York City Ballet, and subsequently the New York City Opera, would not be completed until the following year. Philip Johnson had designed the New York State Theater to accommodate primarily dance but also musical theater, which included operetta and grand opera. The design team and the Center's board also assumed the theater would be available to visiting troupes from a variety of disciplines.

Lincoln Center's organizers had discussed including musical theater, in their view a uniquely American art form, within the performing arts complex. It was not until the early 1960s, however, that any meaningful action was taken. At that point, William Schuman, the newly appointed president of Lincoln Center, emerged as a great champion of the idea. He began by discussing the idea with leading figures in the field, and the Center's executives went on record in September 1962 in support of creating a musical theater constituent. They authorized Schuman to pursue it further, provided the Center "could not be expected to provide the necessary financing for the musical theater."[1]

William Schuman, president of Lincoln Center from 1962 to 1968.

The following month, Schuman reported that Richard Rodgers—the composer of some of the American theater's best-loved musicals, such as *Pal Joey*, *Oklahoma!* and *The Sound of Music*—had agreed to head the new constituent organization.[2] According to Schuman, "I had thought we should do something that had some creative cast to it. Richard Rodgers was a very close friend of mine. All during my youth, I had been a great fan of his. . . . I went to Dick and said, 'What about forming the Music Theater of Lincoln Center to play the New York State Theater with revivals of famous musicals?' He accepted, and we formed the Music Theater at Lincoln Center."[3]

Officially recognized as a constituent in 1963 with Rodgers as its head, the Music Theater agreed to become a tenant of the State Theater once it was completed. This "mixed-use" house ultimately would present problems for each of its resident companies. The size of the orchestra pit—which the architect had enlarged to accommodate the ballet—presented particular difficulties for musical theater. Two rows of temporary seats needed to be added at the front of the house to bring the audience closer to the stage. In addition, a sound-amplification system would have to be installed to accommodate vocal music and the spoken word. These alterations were accomplished just in time for the hall's partially televised opening on April 23, 1964, which included a scene from Rodgers & Hammerstein's *Carousel* as part of the festivities.

Music Theater's organizers hoped, at least initially, to present two revivals each summer at Lincoln Center. Summer presentations in New York had never been particularly successful for any of the performing arts. However, the thinking was that Lincoln Center's air-conditioned halls might provide an irresistible allure during the hot summer months. The Music Theater opened in July with a revival of Rodgers & Hammerstein's *The King and I*, followed by a production of Franz Lehar's operetta *The Merry Widow* in August. In his positive review of *The King and I*, the critic Herbert Kupferberg said, "The only question is whether people will turn out in numbers for a musical revival in the summer months."[4] Yet the box office that summer was exceptionally good, and the future of summer musicals at Lincoln Center seemed promising.

Despite the State Theater's acoustical problems and the logistical challenges arising from three companies sharing the same facility, Music Theater at Lincoln Center persevered. The critics and audiences lauded its productions, which included such favorites as

Kismet, *Annie Get Your Gun*, and *South Pacific*. Its affordable ticket prices attracted large audiences to Lincoln Center, many for the first time. Thus, while some people at Lincoln Center had objected to including American musical theater within the pantheon of the performing arts, Music Theater was certainly a success from the programming point of view. "The cachet of Lincoln Center, of course, had a great deal to do with audience interest, advance interest and appeal," said Henry Guettel, Rodgers's son-in-law and the general manager of the Music Theater from the summer of 1964 through early 1967. "It was an exciting time. I've rarely had more fun than I had at Lincoln Center. . . . It was wonderful, the music was wonderful, the motivations were brilliant, and the desire for perfection was pervasive."[5]

Under Guettel's leadership, Music Theater branched out, sending touring companies of its musicals on the road. In addition, to encourage new talent, it sponsored staged readings of "exploratory" musicals in the basement of the Forum Theater of the Vivian Beaumont Theater. Guettel believed that one of those productions, *Berlin's Mine*, dealing with that tragic and divided city after World War II, might have served as an inspiration for Kander & Ebb's subsequent hit musical *Cabaret*.[6] Music Theater also produced concerts, beginning with "George Gershwin's Theater" at Philharmonic Hall, an enterprise that both audiences and critics enjoyed.

Artistically, no one could have asked for more. Musicals were expensive to mount, however, and Music Theater, despite its healthy grosses and enthusiastic audiences, operated in the red during its first two seasons.[7] Music Theater board chairman Hoyt Ammidon attributed this to the brevity of the summer season, which was limited by contract with the New York State Theater, and huge losses incurred by the touring companies.[8] The following year, though, its production of *South Pacific* proved so successful that, unexpectedly, the Music Theater ended the 1967 season with a surplus.[9] Yet the Music Theater soon found itself caught up in Lincoln Center's financial crisis of the late 1960s, which required management to cut programs and revisit its programming policies. Rodgers was forced to cancel the 1970 summer season.

Several factors contributed to his decision. One observer summarized them at the time: "There was the long strike that postponed the start of the season of the Metropolitan Opera Company. So, the opera season was extended, tying up its Lincoln Center home at the time when it normally would have housed an engagement of the American Ballet Theatre. Rodgers had planned a revival of *The Music Man* starring Sammy Davis Jr. Faced with legal problems if it could not honor its ballet commitment, the Center bigwigs gave Rodgers very short notice to guarantee his occupancy of the State Theater. Contract matters with the ever-busy Davis could not be resolved in time. So, the State Theater was assigned to the ballet company."[10] Facing a deficit, lacking a healthy subscriber base, and unable to raise the money necessary to sustain itself, the Music Theater of Lincoln Center first became inactive and then, in 1974, officially disbanded as a Lincoln Center constituent.[11]

Years later, musical theater returned to the New York State Theater as a distinct programming component. In 1986, the New York City Opera (NYCO), then led by Beverly Sills, received a $5 million grant from the philanthropist and longtime Lincoln Center board member Lawrence A. Wien to produce classic American musicals. For the next five years, through the 1990 season, NYCO mounted revivals during its own spring season of such favorites as Lerner & Loewe's *Brigadoon*, Meredith Willson's *The Music Man*, and Rodgers & Hammerstein's *The Sound of Music*. While these five seasons were not altogether successful from a critical point of view, the public responded well to them, underscoring the validity of the initial impulse to include American musical theater among the performing arts at Lincoln Center. In subsequent years, City Opera, under Christopher Keene's direction, presented musical revivals as part of the company's regular repertory. In 1991, for instance, it offered Frank Loesser's *The Most Happy Fella*, and in 1996 it mounted a production of Stephen Sondheim's *A Little Night Music* and a second revival of *Brigadoon*.

Lincoln Center Theater also produced a number of American musicals: popular revivals of *Anything Goes* and *Carousel*; original new musicals, such as *My Favorite Year* and *Parade*; and the well-received dance musical *Contact*, which opened in March 2000. In addition, songs from American musicals were performed as part of Lincoln Center's American Songbook series beginning in 1999. Even though the Music Theater had been dissolved as a constituent in 1974, much of its spirit and thrust remained evident in the contemporary programming at Lincoln Center.

The Film Society of Lincoln Center

The idea of including film in some way at Lincoln Center surfaced almost at the beginning. "It had been my strong feeling that Lincoln Center could have been erected a hundred years ago, with all the constituents in place, and the only new constituent that could be added was film, because film was a twentieth-century art form that hadn't existed before," William Schuman, the former president of Lincoln Center, reminisced in 1990. "I was determined to try to get film into the program at Lincoln Center. . . . I remember various persons saying that film was not a lively art, and I countered with the fact that it was livelier than lots of things that went on. The objection that was made to film was that 99 percent of it was junk. I absolutely agreed with that—and that 99 percent of music, theater, literature, and any other art is also junk; that you don't judge an art by the part that's not successful or not distinguished; and that this could be a great addition to the offerings of the Center. Eventually my view prevailed."[12]

In late 1962, Schuman spoke with Amos Vogel, an Austrian-born film aficionado, about doing something to change the situation. Within a matter of months, Vogel negotiated a collaborative arrangement with Richard Roud of the London Film Festival and launched the first New York Film Festival. Cosponsored by the British Film Institute, which ran the London festival, and the Museum of Modern Art, which had operated a successful film program for many years, Lincoln Center staged its event in Philharmonic Hall in September 1963. Although it was a popular success that attracted huge crowds, some criticism surfaced—mainly involving programming choices that were made, which Vogel believed could be addressed by establishing film as a continuing presence at the Center. "I felt that Lincoln Center needed an all-around, yearlong film center—meaning a film constituency with its own performances every single day, several performances of all kinds of films—because I felt it would open the way for other people to be shown whose films had not been selected for the festival."[13]

Though it lost money—a perennial problem for performing arts organizations—the festival's popular success encouraged those who wanted to provide film with an institutional base. A major reason was that this art form attracted a new and different audience to the Center. It also had a constructive effect on film as an art form, according to Schuman. Putting this potential constituent on a firm financial foundation became the first order of business. An official committee set to work, chaired by William F. May, the president of the American Can Company, and organized by Martin E. Segal, a prominent New York civic activist, film buff, and friend of William Schuman, who would become the Center's chairman in 1981. "The film activity was badly in debt," recalled Segal, "so we had to work out a compromise for paying off the debt."[14] He took principal responsibility for establishing the Film Society of Lincoln Center as an entity distinct from the New York Film Festival,[15] and May headed the fund-raising effort, which wiped out the debt to Lincoln Center and laid the basis for future financial stability.

In 1969, May and Segal organized the Film Society to operate the festival. Subsequently, it initiated new projects and programs, including an annual gala tribute to screen legends, who, over the years, have included Fred Astaire, Gregory Peck, and Bette Davis. The Society's very first gala, in 1972, honored silent-screen star Charlie Chaplin. The choice of Chaplin took some courage, since the actor had been barred from traveling to the United States for more than twenty years because of his political views. It was considered a great coup to get him, a feat that Segal managed with diplomatic aplomb. "The gala," which he cochaired with David Rockefeller Jr., "really established the Society as something more than just the New York Film Festival,"[16] recalled Segal.

That same year, the Society—with the help of a grant from the Rockefeller Brothers Fund and the cosponsorship of the Museum of Modern Art's Film Department—instituted its New Directors/New Films series. "This partnering with the museum was a very good idea," said Amos Vogel, "bringing them together, a valuable addition to the New York film scene."[17] It provided a venue for directors who were perhaps considered too daring or who had too little box-office appeal because they were completely new. Here was a place where their films could be shown. New Directors/New Films, according to Joanne Koch, the then executive director of the Film Society, "is a very idyllic collaboration, amazingly so."[18] The Film Society raised the money and administered the program, which was screened at the Museum of Modern Art every year.

The Film Society became an official constituent of Lincoln Center in 1974, but its goal of establishing a year-round presence at the Center had to wait a number of years to be achieved. There had been an attempt in the early 1970s to establish just such a program in the downstairs theater at the Vivian Beaumont, but theater management proved unwilling to cede that space. The Center's decision to construct the Rose Building in the mid-1980s renewed the possibility of a permanent presence on campus. Alfred Stern, the then president of the Society, helped to secure a $1.2 million grant from the Walter Reade Foundation, and the dream was on its way to becoming a reality.

Designed primarily for film but also to serve as a recital hall, the

Walter Reade Theater was the first new concert space added at Lincoln Center since the complex was completed in 1969.[19] It opened in December 1991 and garnered admiring reviews. Vincent Canby, the *New York Times*'s main film critic at the time, suggested that it "may well be the most inviting new movie house to open in New York in years. . . . It's a handsome, comparatively small (268 seats) but spacious house of nervy character, seemingly unencumbered by the sobriety and uplift of its high-art context." He added that it was successful in the way it "bridges the gap between art and commerce."[20] Even the popcorn, brownies, and soda sold at the concession stand made news. "The decision to sell popcorn . . . First of all, it was good initial publicity, because a Lincoln Center venue where popcorn was being sold put a whole different connotation on it, and made it a much friendlier place,"[21] recalled Joanne Koch.

The addition of this first-rate theater drew new audiences to Lincoln Center and secured the future success of the Film Society. "We are filling a niche by showing these films," Koch said. "We will continue to do diverse programming, to make it as unique as we can and strike that balance between what is socially and politically correct and what is great art. That's going to be the challenge over the next five years." Moreover, the Walter Reade Theater became the city's preeminent venue for new international cinema. "The need for the Walter Reade is much greater than it was when we started building it," said Koch, "because there are very few repertory houses left. Foreign films with subtitles do well in Walter Reade, because people don't like to watch them at home. No one does this kind of programming the way we do. The Film Society's programs bring a lot of people to Lincoln Center, people who might not otherwise come here."[22]

In June 2003, after thirty-two years at Lincoln Center, Joanne Koch retired and was succeeded by Claudia Bonn, who had served the Film Society first as the director of development and then as the director of administration and development. Under her, the Film Society of Lincoln Center continues its ambitious year-round

New York Film Festival patrons gather outside Alice Tully Hall, October 1982, the festival's twentieth anniversary.

programming in the Walter Reade Theater; sponsors the New York Film Festival every fall; showcases the newest and some of the most important works by directors from around the world in New Directors/New Films; organizes its annual spring gala tribute to a distinguished film artist; and publishes *Film Comment*, a unique magazine about movies and movie people.

Soon, as part of Lincoln Center's 65th Street Redevelopment Project, the Film Society of Lincoln Center will have two new screening rooms and an amphitheater-style space where it will sponsor lectures, symposia, and educational programming, expanding yet again its popular roster of offerings.

The Chamber Music Society of Lincoln Center

In an interesting twist of fortune, Lincoln Center's Chamber Music Society became for a time the victim of its own success. In September 1969, when Charles Wadsworth, its first musical director, took to the podium for the premiere performance, there were few venues in New York City where the full spectrum of chamber music repertory could be heard. "Most places that presented chamber music, such as the Metropolitan Museum or Town Hall, presented string quartets," said Wadsworth. "My idea was to give the people works they never would have heard before. I felt there was an enormous amount of repertory that, if put together properly, would fascinate the public."[23]

Wadsworth, an accomplished pianist, chamber musician, and accompanist, had joined with William Schuman and the members of the Lincoln Center Committee on Chamber Music (Alice Tully, Sampson Field, Frank Taplin, and Edward R. Wardell) in 1965 to create the Chamber Music Society of Lincoln Center to fill a very important gap in the Center's offerings. Wadsworth and his colleagues planned to establish a resident ensemble that would work with invited guest artists. "I also felt it was crucial that one of our mandates must be to enlarge the chamber repertoire," he said, "and to begin right away a strong commissioning program, which we could prepare to the best of our ability and present."[24]

To avoid competing with other Lincoln Center resident companies, particularly for donors whose loyalties might be divided, the Chamber Music Society carefully defined the scope of its repertoire, eschewing pieces with multiple musicians on one part that could be considered orchestral in nature.

The inaugural concert at Alice Tully Hall could not have been received more enthusiastically. The new hall—reportedly the first built especially for chamber music anywhere in the United States—delighted everyone and was, as the *New York Post* critic exclaimed, a "source of joy for its tasteful beauty, its fine acoustics and its distinctive purpose."[25] The concert, which included Bach's Trio Sonata in C for two violins and continuo, Schumann's *Dichterliebe*, and Schubert's Quintet, Opus 163, was greeted with similar praise. "What [the audience] could not have anticipated was how well they would be served by the newly organized Chamber Music Society of Lincoln Center," wrote Irving Kolodin in *Saturday Review*. "If this personal standard is one to which his [Wadsworth's] group will adhere, its future couldn't be more promising."[26]

And so, in Alice Tully's commodious new hall, the collective dream became a reality: a first-class ensemble performing a wide range of material for a loyal audience. It started small, with only sixteen concerts the first year, the idea being "Let's prove ourselves, let's build up our membership and get our finances in order."[27] By 1972, the Society was in good enough financial shape to be elected an official constituent of Lincoln Center. Eventually, the Society's season comprised ninety concerts.

Including chamber music in Lincoln Center's performing arts mix had first been contemplated in the late 1950s, and a hall had been included in the original master plan.[28] As Alice Tully, a former opera singer and vocalist and a champion of chamber music, later recounted, "In 1958, my cousin, Arthur Houghton, Jr.—one of the ten founders of Lincoln Center—invited me to lunch and asked me if I would be interested in helping that new project called Lincoln Center for the Performing Arts. They wanted some help with the chamber music hall. . . . I had a wonderful feeling when he asked me that. 'Oh, Arthur, I can't think of anything I'd rather do.' I wanted to know the name of and about the acoustician to be sure the hall would be successful. When I heard who it was [Heinrich Keilholz], I consented to give my name."[29] Alice Tully, who was intimately involved in every aspect of the design, the construction, and the interior decoration of the hall that would bear her name, became the Chamber Music Society of Lincoln Center's first chairman of the board, a post she held for some twenty years.

Charles Wadsworth, the first director of the Chamber Music Society of Lincoln Center.

Throughout the 1970s and well into the 1980s, the Chamber Music Society enjoyed unprecedented success. Its audience, although somewhat older and by some accounts heavily Middle European in origin, filled the hall to near 100 percent capacity year after year. "I think we were on the cutting edge of the chamber music revolution, which then spread widely all over the place," said Frank Taplin, a founder, a longtime board member, and the president of the Society from 1969 to 1974. "The Chamber Music Society had a programming concept that was quite original—a nucleus of artists, augmented by guest artists, doing a wide range of the literature."[30]

Charles Wadsworth had a winning way with audiences. Together with the first-class ensemble he had recruited, he not only brought chamber music new prominence but also inspired the creation of numerous chamber music organizations around the country. "Charles Wadsworth has shown how small ensembles can attract big audiences," said one reviewer. "Wadsworth's sense of the enchantment buried in chamber music literature, his knack for programming it and for finding the right performers to rejoice in it, has created a boom in chamber music."[31] Wadsworth succeeded in bringing some of the world's great soloists—including Frederica von Stade, Dietrich Fischer-Dieskau, and Beverly Sills—to perform with his resident ensemble. According to the *New York Times*'s music critic Bernard Holland, Wadsworth "did not simply present chamber music; he sold it. His particular talent was to create original programs in which the music—though not necessarily heavy with substance—almost always had enough charm to please audiences and enough character to justify its presence."[32]

But success inevitably invites imitation. The Chamber Music Society began to tour during the 1971–72 season, and Wadsworth realized "that we were having a major impact on the rest of the country, insofar as chamber music was regarded. . . . I was getting calls from St. Louis, from Atlanta, different cities where they had symphony orchestras, and they would say, 'We are forming a chamber music society, patterning this society after the Lincoln Center Chamber Music Society. Is that all right with you? Will you tell us how you've gone about doing certain things?'" By the late 1980s, nearly every major city in the United States had some kind of chamber ensemble and ample audiences attending their concerts. The competition reportedly hurt the Society's box office. "Perhaps we paid the price a little bit for our success," said Wadsworth, "because other organizations—the 92nd Street Y and others—came in and established very interesting programs."[33]

This issue became particularly pertinent as Wadsworth, turning sixty, prepared to retire in 1989—a date that coincided with the Society's twentieth anniversary. For many people, Wadsworth *was* the Society; he would be a tough act to follow.

At Wadsworth's farewell concert, Mayor Edward I. Koch presented him with the Handel Medallion, New York City's highest official cultural honor. The program "was like opening birthday presents," said Wadsworth. It consisted of Ravel's Introduction and Allegro, Poulenc's Sextet for Piano and Winds, and Schubert's Quintet in C, which subscribers had requested.[34]

The Society selected Fred Sherry—a cellist and conductor and a member of the ensemble since 1984—as Wadsworth's successor. Sherry's enthusiasm for contemporary music was not wholeheartedly embraced by the Society's longtime subscribers, and perhaps he attempted to make his mark too quickly. Sherry's difficulties increased when he removed four of the Society's original musicians and accepted the resignations of seven others. He also made substantial changes in the roster of resident artists. Some critics and musicians applauded his approach, but the public's response was mixed. Difficult economic times only exacerbated the situation: during Sherry's two-year tenure as artistic director, the Society's box office dropped and so did the ranks of its faithful. Nevertheless, Sherry did provide the ensemble with "a more consistent level of polish and flexibility than it had been known for," wrote one critic, "and after several years away from the studio, it began making recordings again."[35]

Fred Sherry resigned in June 1991, and Charles Wadsworth feared for the future. "Unless the Society is able to come up with some remarkably strong, charismatic person who will have a huge impact—who will make the people want to come back into that hall to the concerts," he said, "there is the danger, at the moment, that something rather drastic could happen."[36] Clarinetist David Shifrin, a member of the ensemble for three years and an experienced administrator, took up the post the following year.

Shifrin brought great energy and a clear set of goals to the job. He wanted to increase the number of artist members and to continue to perform the body of great chamber music literature, but he also intended to survey twentieth-century music.[37] Shifrin faced several difficult challenges, not the least of which was reinvigorating the Society's box office and membership. Fortunately, he "had a good deal of experience putting programs together and building something of interest to audiences, attracting them," remarked Taplin.[38]

Shifrin accomplished much of what he had set out for himself. Programmatically, he expanded the Society's reach, and he reconstituted the Society's traditional audience. Perhaps most important, he expanded the conventional definition of chamber music in an effort to attract new audiences. For example, in October 1997, the opening concert of the season featured instrumentation that included a banjo and a mandolin, and packed Alice Tully Hall.[39]

And, in 2002, the Society collaborated with dancer/choreographer Bill T. Jones in an evening of new dances to music by Beethoven, Shostakovich, Gyorgy Kurtag, and Mendelssohn. Shifrin said at the time, "The fear of doing this kind of program is that you could become a pit orchestra for a dance company. But from the very beginning, the idea was collaboration, and Bill has been enormously respectful of the music and the musicians. This is very different from what we've done in the past, but in many ways it fits right into our mission: We're dedicated to bringing new people into the world of chamber music, and expanding the definition of what chamber music is."[40]

Under Shifrin, in addition to its performances at Alice Tully Hall, the Society embarked on national and international tours, gave nationally televised broadcasts on *Live from Lincoln Center* and on Public Radio International's *Chamber Music New York*, and appeared regularly on National Public Radio's *Performance Today*. The Society continued to commission new works, built a large and critically acclaimed discography, and developed educational programs reaching thousands of students around the tri-state area. And its CMS Two program engaged outstanding chamber music musicians for two-year residencies. It also engaged in collaborative efforts with other Lincoln Center constituents—such as *Der Golem*, which it presented in collaboration with the Film Society—which served to infuse the seasons with special excitement. And, with programming aimed specifically at younger concertgoers, he succeeded in drawing in new audiences.

Any fear for the well-being of the Chamber Music Society

proved unfounded. In Shifrin, the Society had acquired an effective leader and a world-class musician who successfully bridged the gap between past and future. In its musicians, the Society could claim the nation's premier repertory chamber music ensemble.

After twelve years as artistic director, Shifrin stepped down in 2004. After an extensive international search, the Chamber Music Society announced on June 14, 2004, that it had appointed the cellist David Finckel and the pianist Wu Han, two well respected classical musicians, to succeed him. "Widely recognized for their initiatives in expanding audiences for classical music and for guiding the careers of countless young musicians,"[41] they seemed a perfect fit for the Chamber Music Society, said Norma Hurlburt, the executive director of the Chamber Music Society. They "are not only brilliant performing artists, but true innovators. They bring great imagination to their programming and communicate a great sense of excitement about the repertoire." David Finckel and Wu Han, who are a married couple, were scheduled to present their first programmed season in 2006–2007.

Lincoln Center Theater

Possibly the most dramatic tale in Lincoln Center's history belongs to its theater component. The story rivals the many onstage dramas that have played in Eero Saarinen's sleekly beautiful modernist building, the Vivian Beaumont Theater. It is a saga of clashing ambitions, lost opportunities, and, finally, resurrection and triumph.

Lincoln Center's founders considered drama—the art of the spoken word—essential to the fulfillment of their vision for the performing-arts complex. To that end, they formed a drama committee in late 1956 to think through the artistic concept of a theater constituent. "The decision to include the art of spoken drama in Lincoln Center had been relatively easy to make. To find an appropriate institution to sponsor the drama proved far more difficult. The center needed an organization that would become, in its field, a counterpart to the Metropolitan Opera Association and the Philharmonic-Symphony Society,"[42] with a financially stable institutional framework and a dedication to artistic advancement.

The concept envisioned by the theater's first directors, the seasoned theater professionals Robert Whitehead and Elia Kazan, called for a resident repertory company that would make the Lincoln Center campus its home. The company, it was hoped, would be akin to the Old Vic in England, performing a rotating selection of plays in repertory each season and thus filling a notable vacuum in the American theater.[43]

The Lincoln Center board accepted this idea and charged Kazan and Whitehead with building the theater constituent, which it at first called the Lincoln Center Repertory Theater, and the institutional base that would sustain it. Construction delays on the Saarinen building forced them to stage their first two seasons downtown, beginning in January 1964 with Arthur Miller's *After the Fall*, in a temporary structure in Washington Square Park. By the end of the second season, the company was struggling financially, due primarily to poor attendance during the summer months and the high cost of its productions.

By the time Saarinen's building opened in October 1965, Whitehead and Kazan had stepped down. They were replaced by Jules Irving and Herbert Blau, codirectors of San Francisco's Actor's Workshop. Their choice, wrote *Newsweek*, "astounded and delighted the serious theater world,"[44] and they soon filled the upstairs Vivian Beaumont Theater and the smaller downstairs space, then called the Forum Theater, with a variety of plays, readings, and experimental productions. These sometimes met with criticism in the press, however, beginning with their very first production, *Danton's Death*, starring James Earl Jones. Blau left after two years on the job, but Irving remained.

By 1972, mounting financial deficits threatened the theater's operations. "Both the Beaumont and the Forum can play to capacity," explained Irving, "and we still lose money."[45] The theaters were very costly to operate. Consequently, the Repertory's season proved inordinately expensive. In addition, this made it difficult to rent the theaters to outside companies when the Repertory Theater was not in residence. Also, according to Amyas Ames, the then chairman of Lincoln Center, the theater's board just "did not produce enough money."[46]

Lincoln Center had contemplated a financial rescue the previous year. At the board's request, City Center—already operating the New York State Theater on behalf of its City Opera and City Ballet companies—prepared a $1.2 million bailout plan. In effect, City Center offered to take control of the theater and turn it into a multi-use facility housing a smaller theater for drama but also (and primarily) three movie theaters, offices, and a restaurant—an American version of Paris's Cinémathèque.[47] Lincoln Center considered the plan but ultimately decided to retain the theater.

Faced with the cancellation on financial grounds of the remainder of the Forum's 1972 season, Jules Irving resigned in protest.[48] The search for a new artistic director produced the charismatic and outspoken Joseph Papp, the head of the New York Shakespeare Festival. "In a major change of artistic policy at the Center, Mr. Papp will emphasize the production of new American plays instead of revivals at the Vivian Beaumont Theater and will turn the 299-seat Forum Theater into a year-round home for Shakespeare," the *New York Times* reported.[49]

The Center's drama constituent was restructured and renamed the New York Shakespeare Festival at Lincoln Center. Papp began his tenure on November 8, 1973, with a production of David Rabe's *In the Boom Boom Room*, a portrait of a go-go dancer that pleased critics. It garnered a Tony nomination in 1974 but proved unsettling to more than a few Lincoln Center theatergoers. After four uneasy years—having mounted many controversial productions, including Rabe's *Streamers* and Miguel Pineiro's *Short Eyes*, as well as more traditional offerings such as Anton Chekhov's *The Cherry Orchard* and Bertolt Brecht and Kurt Weill's *The Threepenny Opera*—Papp pulled out of Lincoln Center.

Now lacking a resident organization and unable to attract a commercial producer (by that time its costs were nearly double those of a comparable Broadway theater and its grosses only marginally higher), the house went dark in August 1977.[50] As the theater's landlord, Lincoln Center considered several options. The board determined that a new organization was needed to take over the theater, one with a new board of directors—and thus possible new sources of funds—and strong artistic leadership. Lincoln Center also set about the arduous task of renegotiating contracts with the stagehands' union and Actors' Equity to lower operating expenses and thus make the theater a more viable operation.

In late 1978, Richmond Crinkley—then with the American National Theater Association and a founder of the Folger Shakespeare Theatre in Washington, D.C.—joined the Beaumont. First as a consultant and then as executive director, he was charged with creating a new organization, to be known as the Lincoln Center Theater Company. Crinkley established a five-person directorate to, wrote Mel Gussow in the *New York Times*, "ensure that the Beaumont reflects the full spectrum of the theater, rather than just one viewpoint."[51] The unions agreed to new contracts that same year.

But that was not the end, or even the beginning of the end, of the story. The Vivian Beaumont Theater had always been a controversial venue from the day *Danton's Death* opened on its stage in 1965. The architect Eero Saarinen, in collaboration with the theater designer Jo Mielziner, had created an intimate theater with maximum flexibility—it permitted both a thrust and a proscenium stage—and filled it with sophisticated technical stage and lighting equipment. Its high rake and limited sight lines made some productions difficult to mount. There were also complaints about the acoustics, both from the audience and from actors onstage. Crinkley firmly believed that the Beaumont's problems had an adverse effect on repertory and audience receptiveness, and he championed a complete renovation.[52] Yet he did proceed to mount one three-play season of productions beginning in the fall of 1980, three years after Papp's departure. *The Philadelphia Story* opened the season in the upstairs theater, followed by *Macbeth* and Woody Allen's *The Floating Light Bulb*. In addition, a festival of new one-act American plays was presented in the downstairs space, by that time renamed the Mitzi E. Newhouse Theater.

In April 1981, in the midst of its first (and what would turn out to be its only) season of productions under Crinkley, the theater accepted a $4 million grant from the Fan Fox and Leslie R. Samuels Foundation for the intended renovation, which was proffered subject to the Beaumont's board raising the additional $1.5 million that might be required.[53] The theater closed at the end of the 1980–81 season; construction was scheduled to be completed by the end of the summer of 1982. Among the desired changes were gutting the interior and turning it into a proscenium theater, making the aisle gradient less steep, adding fifty seats, improving sight lines, and relocating the box office.[54]

I. M. Pei was hired as the architect, and Dr. Cyril Harris, who was working simultaneously on the renovation of the New York State Theater, was engaged as the acoustician. According to Harris, he and Pei came to an impasse over plans,[55] and Pei resigned in early 1982. By the time the theater was ready to proceed with its new design team—Hardy Holzman Pfeiffer Associates as architects and Christopher Jaffe of Jaffe Acoustics as the acoustician—in early November 1982, there was growing concern that the theater might be unable to finance the overage. The Fan Fox and Leslie R. Samuels Foundation withdrew its grant to the theater, according to Samuels, because of "the inability of the Vivian Beaumont Company to obtain the funding in the amount of $1,500,000 as provided by the terms of the agreement of July 1, 1981, for its possible use in the reconstruction of the Vivian Beaumont Theater,"[56] although it left open the possibility that the grant could be renegotiated once the Beaumont's board had a completed architectural study and a proposed plan of action. For its part, the Beaumont's board reaffirmed its belief that it could raise the necessary funds once its design plan was in place and it was ready to proceed with renovations.[57]

In December 1982, the theater's board, having studied the matter, voted to eliminate the thrust stage entirely and proceed with a proscenium-only theater, believing it would "correct sight line and acoustical problems, and provide a better financial operation through compatibility with other stages and reduced overhead costs."[58] A theater liaison committee, consisting of the board members W. Barnabas McHenry, Linda LeRoy Janklow, Paul Bauman, and Frederick R. Koch, was appointed to facilitate communications between the theater and Lincoln Center. The Beaumont board continued to adhere to the position that a renovated facility was its first priority, whereas Lincoln Center believed that a season of plays should come first.[59] For Lincoln Center—which funneled significant monies to the theater from both its Consolidated Corporate Fund and its garage receipts—a dark theater was expensive and "an embarrassment,"[60] and an atmosphere of tension and mistrust between the two institutions grew.

On August 23, 1983, the theater's chairman and CEO, Jerome Greene, and its president, W. Barnabas McHenry, both resigned over differences with the majority of their board members, who continued to insist that renovation take precedence over production. The two boards had reached an unpleasant impasse. As a result, Lincoln Center chairman Martin E. Segal persuaded the Lincoln Center board to vote to withdraw its annual $500,000 subsidy—money the theater depended upon to defray rental and maintenance costs—and forbade the theater to use the Lincoln Center name.[61]

"Just at the height of the argument, Alexander H. Cohen and Roy A. Somlyo, the Broadway producers, came to see me," explained Segal. "Cohen and Somlyo said that Peter Brook, the very distinguished theater director, had seen the theater and wanted to do a new version of *Carmen* [*La Tragédie de Carmen*] which had been done in Europe to great success. Peter said he loved the theater and didn't need to make any structural changes; he just needed permission to put dirt on the stage to make it look like a bullring. Of course we agreed, and he opened [in November 1983] without any structural changes, and it was a great success. It made the point that the theater, if used appropriately by someone who had vision and imagination and competence, could do very well."[62]

The successful staging of *Carmen* in Lincoln Center's "controversial and long-neglected Beaumont Theater is brilliantly fulfilled by Peter Brook's fascinating production,"[63] the *Daily News* reported. More important, it demonstrated what some observers already had surmised—that "perhaps the Beaumont's problems aren't so much poor sight lines as insufficient directorial vision,"[64] and that it might be the artistic product, and not the building itself, that determined success or failure in the Vivian Beaumont.

In June 1984, two months after *Carmen* closed, the two boards finally achieved a reconciliation. Under the terms of the accord—negotiated for the theater by Linda LeRoy Janklow, then its acting chairman, and for Lincoln Center by a committee consisting of board members Lawrence A. Wien, Richard R. Shinn, and Gordon J. Davis, and assisted by Center president Nathan Leventhal—the theater would elect a new, independent board chairman (who turned out to be John V. Lindsay, the former mayor of New York). With the approval of the theater's board, the new chairman would issue a detailed analysis of the program and the artistic goals of the theater. Ten new directors, independent of current board members and not committed on the issue of renovation, would join the theater's board. A new artistic director was also to be engaged. Finally, the theater's board would appoint a committee of experts to determine whether—and if so, how—the theater should be renovated. For its part, the Lincoln Center board promised to release the money it had withheld from the theater and agreed to let the theater resume use of the Lincoln Center Theater Company name.[65]

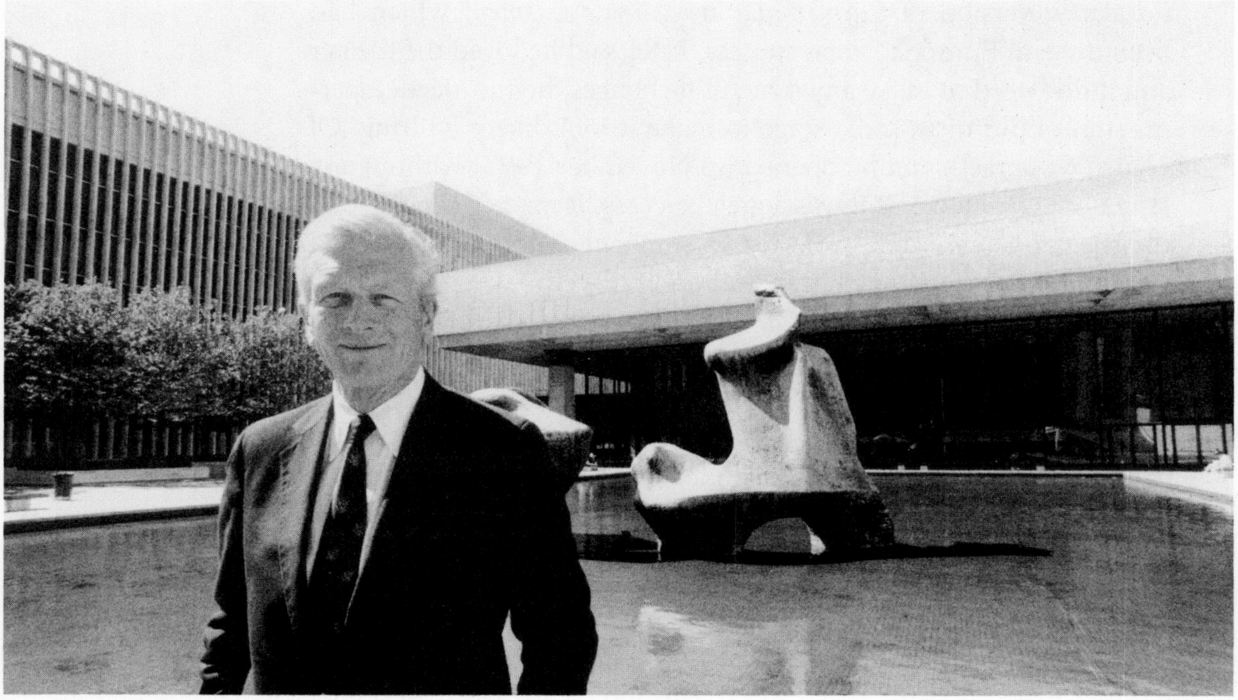

John V. Lindsay, former mayor of the City of New York, pictured in front of the Vivian Beaumont Theater, home of Lincoln Center Theater, of which he was appointed chairman in 1984.

Richmond Crinkley officially resigned in October, expressing his hope that the Beaumont, under new leadership, would again become a vital force in the theater world. "We're having a new beginning, and the whole board wants to get on with it," Janklow told the *New York Times*. "What we care about is building a company, and hopefully we will be able to make it work."[66]

On July 1, 1985, the theater retained Bernard Gersten, "a very experienced, high-minded, intelligent man who knew the ins and outs of theater very well,"[67] as executive producer and Gregory Mosher of Chicago's Goodman Theatre as artistic director. Together with the enthusiastic support and able leadership of John V. Lindsay, they began what Gersten refers to as "the Fifth Ascent of Mount Beaumont."[68]

"We were loath to theorize about what the theater ought to be,"

Gersten remembered. "We said the theater ought to just exist, and it ought to be the best theater we could create. And what would it be? Would it be the theater of classics, a theater of new plays? Would it be a theater of plays or would it be a theater of musicals? Would it be a theater of American works or international works? Our answer was 'all of the above,' and we distilled it to a very simple slogan that we used as our operating slogan: 'Good plays, popular prices.' Let's just make the place lively as a theater."[69]

Gersten and Mosher's first production—two short plays by David Mamet, *Prairie du Chien* and *The Shawl*—opened in the smaller, 300-seat Mitzi E. Newhouse Theater in December 1985. Many critics felt it was a good beginning. Initially, Gersten and

Mitzi (Mrs. S. I.) Newhouse, at a gala in her honor on October 5, 1973, pictured with, left to right: Amyas Ames, chairman of Lincoln Center; Joseph Papp, producer, New York Shakespeare Festival; and New York City mayor John V. Lindsay.

Cast members of Lincoln Center Theater's 1986 production of John Guare's *House of Blue Leaves*. From left: Swoosie Kurtz, John Mahoney, and Stockard Channing surround production director Jerry Zaks, seated.

Mosher intended to open the Vivian Beaumont in the fall of 1986, but the impressive success of their revival of John Guare's *House of Blue Leaves*, which followed the Mamet plays in the Mitzi Newhouse, made them reconsider. Instead, they switched *Blue Leaves* into the 1,000-seat Vivian Beaumont on April 29, 1986. Theater had returned to Lincoln Center. *Blue Leaves* moved to Broadway's Plymouth Theater that fall for an additional six-month run and later became the first Lincoln Center Theater production to be videotaped for broadcast on television.

The rest, as they say, is history. A string of Gersten-Mosher hits followed—*Six Degrees of Separation*, *Anything Goes*, and *Monster in a Box*, to name a few in the upstairs theater; and *Waiting for Godot*, *Sarafina*, and *The Sisters Rosensweig* in the downstairs Mitzi Newhouse—attesting to the wisdom of producing a mix and also to the theater's intrinsic viability as a full-thrust-stage house.

Mosher's term as artistic director expired at the end of December 1991, although he continued as resident director for an additional year. On January 1, 1992, he was officially succeeded as artistic director by Andre Bishop, who came to Lincoln Center from Playwrights Horizons after a successful ten-year tenure there as artistic director. With a substantial grant from Lincoln Center's John D. Rockefeller 3rd Special Purpose Gift Fund, the Beaumont acquired an amenity long wished for: a convertible orchestra pit, located just downstage from the full-thrust stage. Bishop then produced the first new American musical ever mounted in the Beaumont, *My Favorite Year*, and created the position of Director of Musical Theater to encourage the development of more original productions.

Lincoln Center Theater also mounted several productions at Broadway and Off-Broadway houses, such as *Via Dolorosa*, *Mule Bone*, and *The Heiress*. In addition to its full-scale productions, the theater developed new works and young artists through regular play readings, rehearsed workshops of plays and musicals in progress, and began an annual Director's Lab. It also runs an education program that reaches thousands of New York City public school students and publishes the *Lincoln Center Theater Review*, a journal that explores subjects involving its artists and productions.

In recognition of its exceptional success and to commemorate Lincoln Center Theater's twentieth anniversary, the board of Lincoln Center passed a resolution in March 2005 honoring the theater's past and current leadership, including chairmen John Lindsay, Linda LeRoy Janklow, and John Beinecke; artistic directors Gregory Mosher and Andre Bishop; and executive producer Bernard Gersten.[70] By the year 2006, Lincoln Center Theater, in its fifth incarnation—the one that finally worked—had presented a wide variety of plays and musicals at both of its Lincoln Center theaters and at Broadway and Off-Broadway venues, garnering for it hundreds of Tony, Drama Desk, Outer Critics, OBIE, and Grammy nominations and awards. Nowhere in sight were the difficulties of the past. Its new board had made possible $26 million in welcome capital improvements. Millions of theatergoers had enjoyed its productions. "We breathed life into Eero Saarinen's 'glorious structure of a theater,'" said Bernard Gersten. "I think they [the Lincoln Center board of directors] like the fact that the Theater has brought distinction to Lincoln Center, because the Theater is livelier and more with it in a way. They like best of all that we're here, and we're responsible and we do good work."[71]

School of American Ballet

Lincoln Center's 1987 invitation to the School of American Ballet to become a full-fledged constituent fulfilled a dream held by the dance devotee Lincoln Kirstein and the Russian-born dancer and choreographer George Balanchine—that the ballet school they founded would become an integral part of the Lincoln Center family.

Kirstein and Balanchine believed that classical academic ballet could become an American art form, and they established the School of American Ballet in 1934 as "a professional academy to provide dancers as well trained as any other technician, whether it be lawyer, architect or musician. They had a second and no less powerful goal—the establishment of a permanent ballet company that would employ the school's young professionals to dance in a new and growing repertoire."[72] In 1948, under the aegis of the City Center of Music and Drama, they founded the New York City Ballet, with Kirstein as general director and Balanchine as artistic director.

George Balanchine (left) and Lincoln Kirstein, founders in 1934 of the School of American Ballet.

When in 1965 the New York City Ballet became a resident performing company at Lincoln Center's New York State Theater, its educational affiliate, the School of American Ballet, followed to Lincoln Center. Beginning in 1969, it occupied rented studio space in the new Juilliard building. Early discussions of a possible merger with Juilliard's existing dance division to create one educational program had come to naught, but an agreement was reached that leased four of Juilliard's six new dance studios to the School of American Ballet, the remaining two to be occupied by Juilliard's dance program. This shared tenancy was not without strain, as Juilliard worried that the School of American Ballet's presence at Lincoln Center would ultimately displace its own program.[73] In the end, Juilliard's well-regarded but financially beleaguered dance division survived, and for more than twenty years the School of American Ballet enjoyed its tenancy at Juilliard. With the passage of time, though, both institutions, their programs flourishing, increasingly felt the need for additional space.

Through the years, the School of American Ballet had become a leading dance academy, producing some of the nation's finest dancers and choreographers. Competition to be admitted to the program was fierce, but limited rehearsal space and a paucity of decent, affordable housing in New York City presented the School of American Ballet with major challenges. Safe and affordable dorm space was needed if Juilliard and the School of American Ballet were to continue to attract the best students.

In the early 1980s, amid persistent complaints by many of its resident companies about the shortage of space, Center chairman Martin E. Segal appointed a committee, headed by the real-estate developer Frederick P. Rose, to begin planning for a new building on the corner of Amsterdam Avenue and 65th Street. The School of American Ballet expressed interest in becoming a major participant in the new building, where the entire ballet school could be housed, enjoying such amenities as state-of-the-art rehearsal studios and dormitory space for its students. At the urging of Lawrence A. Wien, the Lincoln Center board director emeritus and a patron of the arts, the School of American Ballet formally applied for constituent status in early 1987. Wien told the Center's board of directors he believed that a School of American Ballet constituency would "enhance Lincoln Center's reach, impact and image as a national treasure."[74]

Several issues, however, required resolution first. Lincoln Center's founders had stipulated that each of its constituent organizations must represent a unique area of the performing arts—what was referred to as its "area of primacy"—and that no applicant could be added as a constituent if its activities duplicated those of an existing constituent. Just how the School of American Ballet's activities differed from those of the Juilliard School, of City Center (for the New York City Ballet), and of the Lincoln Center Institute needed clarification and careful articulation. In the end, it was determined that SAB's area of primacy would be "professional education, instruction and training in the field of classical ballet," as distinct from Juilliard's ("professional education, instruction and training in the performing arts"), from City Center's ("the field of ballet, with reference to the creation of ballet works, ballet performances and the use of motion pictures and television with respect to ballet"), and from Lincoln Center Institute's ("developing greater understanding of the arts, including classical ballet, among teachers and students who are not professionals in the field of ballet and have not engaged in professional instruction or in professional study of the arts").[75]

The Juilliard School, City Center, on behalf of the New York City Ballet, and Lincoln Center, Inc., on behalf of the Lincoln Center Institute, all of whom had the right to approve or reject the School of American Ballet's application for constituency status, subsequently did approve it. A few Lincoln Center board members questioned the school's potential draw on the annual Consolidated Corporate Fund and the impact this might have on other constituents, but a study revealed that the change would be insignificant.[76]

On May 4, 1987, immediately preceding a dinner dance at the New York State Theater in honor of Lincoln Kirstein's eightieth birthday, the School of American Ballet and Lincoln Center formally signed legal papers making the school the Center's eleventh resident organization. Chairman George Weissman noted, "The School of American Ballet fills a niche within our total scope of educational programs and presentations by reaching our youngest generation of

Seated: George Weissman (left), chairman of Lincoln Center, with John E. Lockwood, chairman of the School of American Ballet, signing papers declaring SAB an official constituent of Lincoln Center for the Performing Arts, May 4, 1987. Standing, from left: Evelyn M. Finkelstein, Lincoln Center secretary and general counsel; Nathan Leventhal, Lincoln Center president; Natalie Gleboff, executive director, SAB; Alexandra Danilova, faculty, SAB; Peter Martins, chairman of the faculty of SAB; and Rebecca Metzger, SAB student and one of the first two recipients of the Mae L. Wien Award.

performing artists."[77] President Nathan Leventhal added, "Lincoln Center will now enjoy the prestige of including among its offerings the world's finest professional training institution for young dancers."[78] At the dinner, Lawrence A. Wien, who had championed the School of American Ballet's constituency, announced that he had made a $1 million contribution to the newest member of the Lincoln Center family to endow a faculty chair and establish at the school the Mae L. Wien Award, in honor of his late wife.

As an official constituent, the School of American Ballet was eligible to share in both the Center's Consolidated Corporate Fund and its garage revenues. The school also could designate a member of its board to the Lincoln Center board and a representative to the Lincoln Center Council, an advisory body made up of the general managers of the Center's constituent organizations.[79] In addition, it would be represented on the Lincoln Center Council on Educational Programs.

On January 2, 1991, the School of American Ballet moved into its new home in Lincoln Center's Rose Building, where it occupied an entire floor. Its facilities included five large studios, locker rooms and showers, lounges for students and parents, a music classroom, a physical therapy room, and administrative offices. Students now also had a place to live. "We have a huge dormitory tower to assure that the School of American Ballet and Juilliard will continue to attract the best students from around the world and the country, and will provide them with safe, affordable housing so tough to find in the city today,"[80] said Nathan Leventhal. The entire School of American Ballet was now under one roof, in its permanent home on the Lincoln Center campus.

Jazz at Lincoln Center

As Lincoln Center, Inc.'s new Classical Jazz series neared its debut on August 3, 1987, it was obvious that something important was afoot: a three-concert series devoted entirely to this uniquely American art form.

The series reflected the happy convergence of several factors. The previous year, the Lincoln Center board had formally accepted the recommendations of its Committee on the Future to develop programs that would attract new audiences and fill its halls year-round, most particularly Alice Tully Hall, which until that point had not been used for a summer performance.[81] The Center's director of

Visitor Services, Alina Bloomgarden—herself a jazz enthusiast and connected to the jazz community—had been lobbying for a jazz presence at the Center for two years. She found a receptive listener in George Weissman, the chairman of the Center, who had recognized the potential for jazz at Lincoln Center after attending a concert at SUNY–Purchase. "I sat in absolute amazement. First, I enjoyed it so thoroughly; and, secondly, the audience went absolutely wild. Stamping feet, all the things you don't normally see."[82]

Weissman and Center president Nathan Leventhal had asked several staff members, including Bloomgarden, for programming suggestions that would respond to the recommendations of the Committee on the Future. When Bloomgarden received the go-ahead, she approached Wynton Marsalis, the trumpet-playing Juilliard alumnus who, while still in his twenties, had won two Grammys and attracted a large following. Marsalis had been "talking in the media about respecting the classical sensibility of jazz, about recognizing it as a classical music," said Bloomgarden. "I told him we wanted to respond to this vision."[83] The possibility of doing something at Lincoln Center excited Marsalis, and he agreed to put together a three-concert series. "When such a world-renowned performing arts center presents jazz, it is the ultimate acknowledgment of the music's vital place in American culture," said Marsalis. "Lincoln Center can be constructive in ensuring that the high level of musicianship already established in jazz will be maintained."[84]

Jazz had endured what some people referred to as a kind of second-class status in concert halls around the country, including Lincoln Center. True, it was performed in some of the most prestigious halls, but the music establishment had never fully embraced it. Historically, jazz was viewed more as popular music than as a serious art form. Jazz appeared at Lincoln Center as early as 1963 as part of its August Fanfare series, but more typically when an independent promoter rented the Center's halls for one or two nights, or for an independent jazz festival.[85] So the possibility of Lincoln Center producing its own jazz series had particular significance.

Together with Marsalis and Dorthann Kirk of radio station WBGO-FM, Bloomgarden and her Lincoln Center colleagues organized and produced the first season. Classical Jazz, as the three-concert series was known, presented tributes to the jazz greats Thelonious Monk and Charlie "Bird" Parker, along with an evening honoring three great ladies of jazz—Dinah Washington, Bessie Smith, and Mary Lou Williams. "Feeling as I do that the greatness of jazz lies not only in its emotion but also in its deliberate artifice," explained Marsalis, "I have tried in helping to shape Lincoln Center's Classical Jazz series to convey some of the conscious struggle that has gone into the great jazz of the past and to show how it impinges on the present."[86]

The series was a real hit, with both the public and the critics. Tickets sold so well that it was also a financial success.[87] The following month—reaffirming the old adage "timing is everything," or almost everything—the United States Congress passed a resolution recognizing jazz as a rare and valuable national American treasure "to which we should devote our attention, support and resources to make certain it is preserved, understood and promulgated."[88]

Three successful seasons confirmed what everyone suspected at the time—that Lincoln Center should begin to contemplate a larger role for Classical Jazz in its roster of offerings. Gordon J. Davis, a Lincoln Center board member and a former New York City parks commissioner, pressed the Center in this regard, believing as he did that "when you list the great achievements of the modern era in the arts, it's clear that jazz is one of them, right next to the greatest painters and the greatest writers."[89] The idea of eventual constituent status for Classical Jazz began to circulate. The Lincoln Center board appointed a special committee to consider expanding the jazz effort. The committee surveyed other major cultural institutions around the country and could find no serious jazz presence. In its report to the full board, the committee recommended "enriching and enlarging the Center's jazz programming with the eventual establishment of a jazz constituency whose mission would be to recognize jazz's status as a significant and vital art form, and to create an environment in which jazz is studied, experienced and appreciated"[90] by presenting the highest-quality artists and music from all eras.

As an interim step, Lincoln Center formed a classical jazz department. A *New York Times* editorial commended the step. "The new department at Lincoln Center promises to give jazz its proper place in the American artistic pantheon. . . . It will certainly add to the repertoire and luminous reputation of the performing arts center itself."[91]

Achieving full-fledged constituent status meant meeting a set of standards that the founders of Lincoln Center had articulated in 1957:

1. The constituent must be able to provide a needed service in or to the performing arts;
2. It must set and maintain artistic standards of the highest quality;
3. Its professional leadership must gain and hold the respect of experts and of the public;
4. It must have an institutional framework designed to assure continuity and financial stability, a commitment to public service, and a dedication to artistic advancement.[92]

Jazz met the first three of these criteria immediately. The fourth—achieving financial stability to ensure an independent, self-supporting organization—was more difficult, and needed time. The Center believed that an endowment with sufficient capital would do just that, and set the goal of $5 million to launch Jazz at Lincoln Center as a constituent. On December 18, 1995, the day Lincoln Center's board of directors voted to approve its constituency, Jazz had $3.4 million—68 percent—of its endowment goal in hand.[93]

Jazz at Lincoln Center, as the department was known, selected Wynton Marsalis as the artistic director and Rob Gibson, who had headed the Atlanta Jazz Festival, as the executive director and then embarked on the journey to secure financial backing. Gibson, according to Marsalis, brought to Lincoln Center's jazz effort "a

Wynton Marsalis, artistic advisor for Lincoln Center's August 1987 Classical Jazz series, with vocalist Betty Carter.

comprehensive vision of how to use the music as art and how to use it in relation to the community," as well as an appreciation of the "importance of education. He had taste and an understanding of the music. He also had energy and brought that indefatigable energy to the organization."[94]

Immediately, Jazz at Lincoln Center announced a year-round season of activities, including a children's program, film presentations, and a lecture series. The following year, the fifteen-piece Jazz at Lincoln Center Orchestra, led by Marsalis, undertook its first national tour to thirty cities and signed a recording contract with Sony. In 1993, the orchestra flew to France for its first international performance. Jazz established a commissioning program, extending the breadth of the department's activities. Soon there were numerous collaborative undertakings with Lincoln Center constituents, including the Film Society, the New York City Ballet, the Chamber Music Society, and Marsalis's alma mater, Juilliard, as well as a feature performance on *Live from Lincoln Center*.

All was not smooth sailing, however. While the Jazz at Lincoln Center Orchestra was playing to full and appreciative houses both here and abroad, the department—and Marsalis personally—attracted occasional criticism in the press. Some people said the program's clear commitment to "classical jazz" was too exclusionary. Others accused Marsalis of favoritism in his choice of performers and in the selection of musicians who would receive Jazz at Lincoln Center composition commissions. Marsalis himself was criticized for accepting a commission in 1992; he used another in 1994 to write *Blood on the Fields*, for which he received a Pulitzer Prize in 1997.

Yet once the Lincoln Center board approved Jazz at Lincoln Center as a constituent, much of the criticism faded away. Jazz at Lincoln Center had become a permanent fixture both at Lincoln Center and in the world of jazz, where its adherence to a specific view of the genre had become more or less accepted. Wynton Marsalis was widely praised for his musical and leadership abilities. Gordon J. Davis, who had helped to raise \$3.4 million of the organization's $5 million endowment,[95] was elected chairman of Jazz at Lincoln Center on July 1, 1996, the day it became Lincoln Center's twelfth constituent.

The jazz program rapidly expanded to include concerts, national and international tours, residencies, a weekly national radio program, television broadcasts, recordings, publications, an annual high school jazz band competition and festival, a band director academy, a jazz appreciation curriculum for children, advanced training through the Juilliard Institute for Jazz Studies, music publishing, children's concerts, lectures, film programs, and student and educator workshops.

By the spring of 1997, to accommodate this explosion of activity, Jazz at Lincoln Center began to think about having a hall of its own, one designed especially for jazz. Davis and Marsalis looked at possible sites in the Lincoln Center neighborhood. When New York City mayor Rudolph Giuliani announced his intention to include a performing arts center of some kind at the New York Coliseum site at Columbus Circle and 59th Street, Jazz at Lincoln Center applied and subsequently was selected in early 1998. It secured an $18 million pledge from the City of New York—$9 million from the administration and $9 million from the City Council—and an additional $10 million anonymous pledge (later to be revealed as coming from real-estate developer Frederick P. Rose, for whom its new home would be named). Jazz at Lincoln Center's building committee, headed by Rose's son, Jonathan F. P. Rose, selected as its architect the internationally acclaimed Rafael Vinoly. The City of New York chose the Related Companies to serve as developer for the entire Time Warner Center at Columbus Circle, including the Jazz at Lincoln Center component.

In June 2000, plans for the new three-hall facility within the Time Warner Center were unveiled. Of particular interest was the fact that in locating its new hall on 59th Street, Jazz at Lincoln Center was effectively extending the Lincoln Center campus southward by several blocks, thereby redefining the geographical concept of

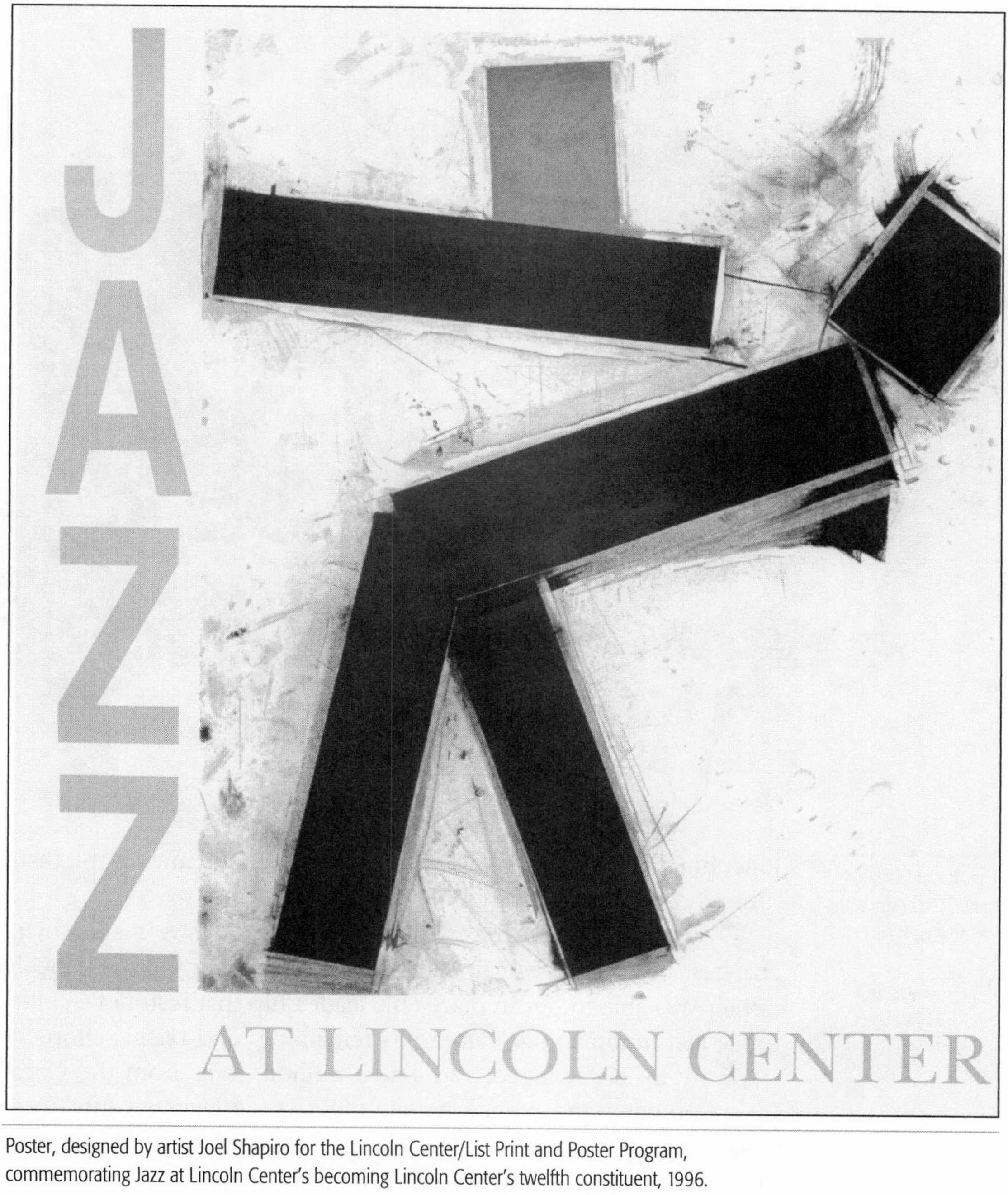

Poster, designed by artist Joel Shapiro for the Lincoln Center/List Print and Poster Program, commemorating Jazz at Lincoln Center's becoming Lincoln Center's twelfth constituent, 1996.

The Jazz at Lincoln Center Orchestra with Wynton Marsalis.

Lincoln Center and acknowledging the enormous impact the institution has had on that neighborhood.

Over the next eighteen months, despite successive management changes, the project remained on track. Eventually, Jazz at Lincoln Center was able to put in place able leadership that restored stability to the institution and galvanized its remaining fund-raising efforts.

Early in 2003, it received a $10 million grant from the Coca-Cola Company and named its late-night space Dizzy's Club Coca-Cola in recognition of this gift. Later that same year, the Atlantic Records founder Ahmet Ertegun made a major gift toward the planned Jazz Hall of Fame to honor inductees and celebrate the history of jazz. An early gift from the Irene Diamond Foundation made possible an education center for classes, workshops, demonstrations, lectures, and student performances. By the time the new Jazz at Lincoln Center facility opened, the City of New York had committed more than $28 million—the increase from its original $18 million pledge due largely to the advocacy of Mayor Michael R. Bloomberg and the generosity of the City Council. In total, Jazz at Lincoln Center raised a remarkable $131 million for its new home.

The Frederick P. Rose Hall, which opened to critical acclaim in October 2004, contained the 1,000-plus seat, multi-use Rose

A performance by the Jazz at Lincoln Center Orchestra with Wynton Marsalis.

Theater, made possible in large part by a generous gift from the Frederick P. and Sandra P. Rose Foundation; the 310- to 500-seat Allen Room, a gift of Allen & Company, for more intimate performances; the 140-seat Dizzy's Club Coca-Cola; the Irene Diamond Educational Center, containing the Edward John Noble Foundation Studio, a gift of the Edward John Noble Foundation; the Louis Armstrong Classroom, a gift of the Louis Armstrong Educational Foundation; and the Ertegun Jazz Hall of Fame.

For its part, Lincoln Center proved to be "very helpful in the realization of Jazz at Lincoln Center's dream for a new home," said current Center president Reynold Levy. "Behind the scenes, we assisted Jazz in many of its efforts, in the things which required Lincoln Center's consent and cooperation."[96] Lincoln Center's creation and nurturing of a jazz presence was a groundbreaking action that, according to Wynton Marsalis, acknowledged "the uniquely American legacy of swing and blues as a history to be valued, an artistic achievement that is on a par with the most magnificent works of Western classical music, dance, theater and film."[97]

Jazz at Lincoln Center's determined evolution into the twelfth Lincoln Center resident organization was a great achievement. "It made a statement about jazz music. It made a statement about Lincoln Center. It's just a remarkable story,"[98] said Nathan Leventhal, as he prepared to retire as president of Lincoln Center in 2000. Marsalis, for his part, echoed these sentiments upon the 2004 dedication of Jazz's new facilities. "The opening of our House of Swing ushers in a new era of jazz," he said. "As artists, we've continued to evolve, but our performing spaces haven't. So we've built a house that really swings with the way jazz works, the way jazz feels and, most of all, the way jazz sounds. The sophisticated sound of the Rose Theater, the communal embrace of the Allen Room, the down-home groove of Dizzy's Club Coca-Cola—each space invites the audience to become one with the music. Now everyone can truly experience the 'democracy' that is jazz."

2

FILLING PROGRAMMING GAPS

Lincoln Center Presents

ALWAYS IN THE MINDS OF LINCOLN CENTER'S FOUNDERS was the idea that in addition to its administrative and real-estate responsibilities, Lincoln Center, Inc.—the umbrella organization under which its resident artistic companies and educational efforts reside—would produce its own programming to fill in gaps in its constituents' offerings. Over the years, these have grown to include an interesting and eclectic array of critically acclaimed artistic and educational endeavors.

Great Performers

William Schuman, the president of Lincoln Center in the 1960s and one of the United States' most celebrated composers, believed that recitals by individual artists should exist at the very heart of the performing arts. Unfortunately, appreciation for this special art form had long been in decline in the United States, and Schuman hoped that Lincoln Center could do something to help revive it. From his conviction sprang Great Performers, which became the Center's longest-running, as well as one of its most popular, series.[1]

With Schuman's active encouragement and participation, Great Performers debuted in the fall of 1965 as a sixteen-concert recital series with a roster of impressive talent. Sharing the bill that first season were, among others, the opera diva Birgit Nilsson, the folksinger Joan Baez, the Chilean pianist Claudio Arrau, the Metropolitan Opera tenor Jon Vickers, and the jazz great Duke Ellington. These concerts were offered as four subscriptions of four recitals each.

Schuman, mindful of the resident companies' wariness about programming competition from Lincoln Center, carefully positioned Great Performers as a supplement to constituents' regular seasonal programs,[2] one that would help to fill Philharmonic Hall when it otherwise would have been dark. Philharmonic Orchestra managing director Carlos Moseley concurred with the artistic intent behind Great Performers. "The big soloists at that time were mainly giving their concerts elsewhere. Their managements were not yet booking them into the new hall. I thought the hall should present a series with great soloists, and I thought that the proper presenter should be Lincoln Center itself. But if Lincoln Center were not to do it, we, the Philharmonic, would have put it on. That was the beginning of Great Performers at Lincoln Center. I am so glad they did, because it was totally right. Then, one after another, many of the great performers decided they could very well perform at Lincoln Center, and have continued to do so."[3]

By the early 1970s, Great Performers included not only classical,

Great Performers banner (1987).

jazz, and folk music, but also rock concerts geared to the singer-songwriter. Four series—two classical and two pop—were offered, and the public snapped up the tickets. Alice Tully Hall was added as an additional Great Performers venue to accommodate "artists whose lack of recognition would normally limit them to bottom billings in rock halls or club dates."[4] In 1974, Great Performers added a series devoted to jazz.

The appearance of the Preservation Hall Jazz Band in April 1976, however, marked the end of Great Performers' "popular" offerings. Growing competition among presenters for popular music name performers and audiences made it too difficult financially for Lincoln Center to continue to showcase this kind of talent. Instead,

Performance artist Laurie Anderson, *Composers' Showcase* at Alice Tully Hall, 1985, part of the Great Performers series.

Great Performers decided to concentrate solely on classical music offerings, which the series packaged in increasingly interesting combinations. For instance, Great Performers offered a series featuring great American orchestras, beginning with the Boston, Cleveland, and Philadelphia symphonies.[5] In the early 1980s, Great Performers added the Art of the Song series in Alice Tully Hall, and, in 1992, it presented a recital by the Manhattan String Quartet in the Film Society of Lincoln Center's new and versatile Walter Reade Theater.

As its name implies, Great Performers featured and indeed had grown to depend on a handful of expensive "name" performers to fill its seats, particularly in Avery Fisher Hall—a practice that increasingly became a financial burden in the late 1980s and early 1990s, as attendance declined.[6] Shortly after Jane Moss arrived at Lincoln Center in late 1992 as vice president for programming, she, Lincoln Center President Nathan Leventhal, chairman George Weissman, and others took a hard look at Great Performers and instituted several new programming initiatives. Among these were composer- or repertoire-focused programming at Alice Tully Hall and the Walter Reade Theater; contemporary music series such as Bang on a Can and the Discovery Series; and nontraditional scheduling, such as Sunday Mornings at 11, a series of one-hour concerts followed by a coffee hour, during which audience members and artists could mingle.[7]

While innovative, these format changes were not completely successful. Ticket sales did not fully recover, subscriptions dropped, and the ever-increasing cost and difficulty of securing star performers all suggested to management the need for a more detailed and rigorous reconsideration of the program. In a New York City marketplace filled with classical music presentations, management decided that "every aspect of the live classical music experience must be reassessed and freshly conceived for a rapidly changing world."[8] With the board's encouragement, Jane Moss and others articulated a revised set of programming objectives for Great Performers to include the development of a new and vibrant artistic profile, distinct from its competitors', that would incorporate audience education, a broadening of repertoire selection, and a strong effort to attract new audiences.

Thereafter, Great Performers expanded to include more repertoire-focused and subject-driven programming, an excellent example of which is the popular What Makes It Great? series, with the composer and conductor Robert Kapilow. It debuted during the 1997–98 season and included musical demonstrations and a question-and-answer period. Great Performers also added more contemporary music and increased its composer commissions and, in 1999, launched its New Visions series to present innovative,

And Furthermore They Bite, Great Performers' Family Musik, with Rob Kapilow at the piano, Alice Tully Hall, 2004.

collaborative works by stage directors, choreographers, musicians, and dancers, many commissioned by Lincoln Center. The following year, the Spoken Word, honoring significant twentieth-century writers, joined Great Performers' growing roster of offerings. Family Musik, a series of interactive family concerts under the Great Performers umbrella and the brainchild of its host, Robert Kapilow, debuted in late 2004 and recently completed its second well-attended season.

Mostly Mozart Festival

> Mozart is the greatest composer of all. . . . [T]he music of Mozart is of such purity and beauty that one feels he merely "found it"—that it has always existed as part of the inner beauty of the universe waiting to be revealed.
>
> —ALBERT EINSTEIN

One genius reflects on another, with the perspective of nearly two hundred years adding to the weight of Einstein's conclusion. Yet only fifteen years after Mozart's death in 1791, a court musician wrote, "He was a meteor on the musical horizon, for whose appearance we were not yet prepared."[9] Admired in his time and in ours, Mozart bequeathed to the ages musical riches in which everyone can delight.

Lincoln Center's air-conditioning—still a technological novelty in the late 1950s and early 1960s, but a welcome blessing in the sweltering humidity of a New York summer—presented both an opportunity and a challenge: how to fill the halls to best advantage programmatically and financially during the summer, when the resident companies were not performing. At that time, the "season" began in mid-September and ended in late May, creating the possibility that the plaza could become an urban desert and the halls a financial drain during June, July, and August. Yet the Center's planners were motivated by more than just the need for additional revenue to keep its operations in the black. One of their primary mandates was to "encourage, sponsor or facilitate performances,"[10] and they intended to do exactly that.

Planning initially focused on Philharmonic Hall, which Schuyler Chapin, Lincoln Center's programming director at the time, once described as a "great big white elephant."[11] Early on, the Center took a gamble, producing a small concert series called August Fanfare in the summer of 1963. Management discovered that an audience for serious music during the summer did in fact exist,[12] and they began thinking about fashioning additional summer programming.

Midsummer Serenades: A Mozart Festival, as it was initially known, proved to be a brilliant collaboration among William Schuman; Chapin; Chapin's young assistant, William Lockwood; and two independent producers, Jay K. Hoffman and George F. Schutz. Midsummer Serenades, which opened in August 1966, featured the New York Chamber Orchestra, distinguished soloists, guest conductors, and chamber music recitals. All tickets were $3, a bargain even then. The *New York Times* heralded the Mozart festival's debut this way: "Twenty-six Mozart programs are being given in Philharmonic Hall this month. If the prospect seems a little stupefying on first consideration, last night's opening concert provided the simple, clear answer: You can't go wrong on Mozart. Provided, of course, you have a shrewdly arranged program, an ensemble of crack instrumentalists, a distinguished soloist and a sensitive conductor. All these were in evidence at the initial event, getting the series off to an excellent start."[13]

Mozart at reasonable prices was a winning formula. Audiences loved it, and the program's popularity convinced Schuman and Chapin that summer programming could generate revenue as well as fill an important programming need. "The lures were informality and affordability. . . . And there was a come-as-you-are atmosphere in the early years that gave the series a lively spirit."[14] Who had the original idea continues to be a matter of dispute, but the choice of Mozart seemed obvious. As Lockwood was quoted as saying, "He wrote enough music of enough variety to sustain such a survey."[15] By 1970, the festival, which already had added works by Haydn and Schubert, became known simply as Mostly Mozart, more accurately reflecting its offerings. Lockwood, who by that time had become the Center's director of programming, was the festival's director and in-house programmer.

Clever advertising campaign slogans during those first years captured the spirit of Mostly Mozart: "Savage Breasts Soothed Here"; "So Don't Put on a Tie"; and "As Much a Fixture of Summer as the Good Humor Man." They challenged New Yorkers and tourists alike: "What would summer be in New York without baseball, outdoor theater, street fairs and, of course, Mostly Mozart? Mostly hot, humid and humdrum. That's what."

What had begun as a four-week festival expanded gradually to five, then six, and finally in 1981 to seven weeks, because the previous seasons' concerts had been mostly standing room only. Yet the festival still had no permanent musical director, and its resident orchestra rotated with visiting chamber music groups. In 1982, to quell criticisms about the orchestra's inconsistency, Lincoln Center appointed Gerard Schwarz—who had debuted with Mostly Mozart as a trumpet soloist in 1977—as the orchestra's permanent conductor.

"There was no music director, no personality," he recalled. "There was nobody instilling a way to play. I knew what it would take to make it into a cohesive orchestra. I also had a lot of curiosity about repertoire."[16] Schwarz and Lockwood, until his departure from Lincoln Center in 1991, spent the ensuing seasons enlivening and enriching the festival. "The biggest problem was not finding the players," said Schwarz, "but making them into a homogenous ensemble that played together as a unit. That's a big issue with an orchestra like ours, which only operates in the summertime. We didn't have a week of rehearsal prior to the opening, nor do we now,

Gerard Schwarz, musical director of Mostly Mozart through 2001.

and it takes a little time for us to learn how to play together again and remember our style."[17]

Together, Schwarz and Lockwood planned each season's programs. "My job was to make a first-class orchestra and to invigorate the repertoire," recalled Schwarz, "not to do the same pieces over and over again. That's not to say we couldn't do the *Jupiter* Symphony every year, but it is to say we could do all the other pieces, too, and some early Mozart operas."[18] Each year, when they added new selections, they would identify them with an asterisk on the season's schedule.

In the summer of 1988, Schwarz and Lockwood added a full week of Haydn, which Schwarz admits to have particularly enjoyed. "In the middle of the all-Haydn week, we had a Haydn Marathon, which began at two in the afternoon and went until ten or eleven at night. We covered a great variety of vocal music, chamber music, and solo works. Many great artists appeared, and it was a wonderfully enjoyable event."[19]

The experimentation continued, including a hugely popular all-star Festival of Fiddlers. Schwarz also insisted on presenting Handel's *Messiah* in German; there were questions about whether it would fly in the summertime—and at the Mostly Mozart Festival, no less—but Schwarz knew his audience. It sold out. Beginning in the summer of 1991, Lincoln Center—with contributions from all of its constituents—marked the bicentennial of the composer's death by performing every Mozart composition over the course of the following year and a half. Beginning that same year, and continuing for the next eight, Mostly Mozart traveled to Tokyo.

Some prominent music critics may have tired of Mostly Mozart after twenty-eight seasons, but its audiences had not, and in 1994, after rumors of its cancellation hit the newspapers, the public made its feelings known. Subsequently, the Center did pare back the festival to its original four weeks, but only to make room for the new Lincoln Center Festival, which debuted in July 1996. Mostly Mozart remained one of the Center's most reliable box-office attractions, having nurtured a faithful audience. Adding immeasurably to the visibility of Mostly Mozart, *Live from Lincoln Center* televised many of its season's opening concerts.

Begun with a resident orchestra rotating with invited chamber groups, Mostly Mozart evolved, under Gerard Schwarz's leadership, into "a showcase for guest conductors and visiting ensembles."[20] Schwarz's retirement at the end of the 2001 season brought turmoil

The Mark Morris Dance Group participated in the first staged event in Mostly Mozart's history, dancing in the New York State Theater to Handel's *L'Allegro, il Penseroso Moderato*, August 2002.

the following year: while awaiting the appointment of a new maestro and amid fears that the new conductor might want to make major changes, the Mostly Mozart Orchestra walked out in July 2002. The four-day strike forced the cancellation of two-thirds of its concerts and was settled by an agreement that called for a three-person panel to review all firing decisions and to participate in the audition process.[21]

In December 2002, Mostly Mozart welcomed the charismatic young French conductor Louis Langrée as its next musical director,

and his success was immediate. "He appears to be the musical shot in the arm that the festival needs," commented one critic. "Langrée and his orchestra seem to have bonded in record time."[22] By 2004—his second season—Langrée was being credited with infusing Mostly Mozart with a new energy and spirit that audiences and critics eagerly welcomed and embraced. For its 2005 season, Langrée and Jane Moss, the Center's vice president for programming, undertook an experiment that proved highly successful: they had Avery Fisher Hall temporarily reconfigured for the Festival, extending the

Louis Langrée, appointed musical director of Mostly Mozart in 2002, with Joshua Bell, violinist, at Avery Fisher Hall, August 2004.

stage thirty feet into the hall and installing courtside seating at the sides and behind the orchestra. This was done to make the listening experience more intimate and to allow the audience, as Langrée explained, "to more fully experience the complexity, the motional nuances and the transcendence rooted in the human experience that lies at the heart of Mozart's genius."[23] Plans were under way to repeat the reconfiguration for the 2006 season, which marks the fortieth anniversary of Mostly Mozart at Lincoln Center.

Under Langrée, Mostly Mozart attendance is up, with many offerings sold out. Langrée and Moss continue to expand and develop new kinds of programming for Mostly Mozart that explores the genius of Mozart, as well as the music of composers who influenced him and of those whom he influenced.

Lincoln Center Festival

Lincoln Center's summer programming efforts began in 1963 with its August Fanfare Series. In 1966, it introduced Midsummer Serenades: A Mozart Festival, later to become known as Mostly Mozart. But Lincoln Center's then president William Schuman had even more in mind for what summer at Lincoln Center could be. He envisioned an international festival of the performing arts "to challenge the notion that summer audiences are less sophisticated than those of winter." Said Schuman, "We are going to provide in gracious, air-conditioned surroundings a series of artistic events that will complement the great outdoor festivals. This vast audience can expect to see and hear the work of some of the most gifted people in the world, not only in standard repertory but also in new works commissioned expressly for the festival by Lincoln Center. Our aim is to establish a festival that can be looked forward to each summer by residents of the greater New York area and by visitors from the country at large and foreign lands."[24]

Schuman asked Schuyler Chapin, the Center's vice president of programming, to put together what would become Festival '67. Chapin traveled to Europe to arrange bookings for what the *New York Times* called "the first [festival] of its kind in the United States, or in the world, to take in all the performing arts in an urban center."[25]

Festival '67 opened on June 12, 1967, and for the next six weeks audiences were treated to performances by musical groups that had never before appeared in the United States, including the Hamburg State Opera, L'Orchestra de la Suisse Romande, and the Bath Festival Orchestra. Also included were two weeks of films from Czechoslovakia and musical compositions commissioned especially for the festival. Poetry readings, recitals, and special events rounded out the two-hundred-performance event, which made use of four Lincoln Center halls as well as off-campus venues. Schuman later reported that while the festival had not been a financial success, it had, in terms of both public attendance and press reception, exceeded his fondest hopes.[26]

The next year, Festival '68 presented an equally eclectic program of music, opera, theater, dance, poetry, and film. Among the groups performing were the Rome Opera; the Théâtre de la Cité from Lyons, France; Atelje 212 from Belgrade; and the Pittsburgh and Boston Symphony orchestras. A poster—commissioned by Lincoln Center as part of the List Poster and Print Program and designed by the artist Allan D'Arcangelo—publicized the festival. Schuman had every reason to believe that he was well on the way toward establishing an annual summer performing arts festival of international significance.[27]

His hopes were dashed, however, on November 18, 1968, when Lincoln Center's board of directors rescinded its earlier agreement to support and finance the upcoming 1969 festival. Festival '68, while a critical and popular success, had lost more money for Lincoln Center than Festival '67 had. The Center's mounting deficits—due in some measure to Schuman's ambitious programming activities, combined with inadequate fund-raising—brought matters to a head. It appeared that Lincoln Center was headed for technical bankruptcy,[28] and the international summer festival fell victim to this crisis.

For many years thereafter, Lincoln Center was reluctant to consider sponsoring another full-blown summer festival, although there were those who believed that New York City, as the cultural capital of the world, could support such an event. Yet Lincoln Center's summer allure remained, and new programming quickly emerged, albeit on a more modest level.

Beginning in 1975, Lincoln Center Out of Doors became a formidable summer presence on campus. Its varied programs, ranging from the traditional to the contemporary, and free of charge to all, attracted a new and different audience to Lincoln Center and lent to the campus an air of bustling excitement. Mostly Mozart had also expanded its season to a full seven weeks by 1981. Then, in 1989, Lincoln Center initiated Midsummer Night Swing, featuring dance band concerts in the plaza that drew enthusiastic crowds to its cool evenings of popular music.

In 1986, Lincoln Center's Committee on the Future recommended additional summer programming to attract new and younger audiences and to make use of the halls that still were often dark from mid-May to mid-September. The committee's report led directly to the creation of two new summer programs that "enhanced the sense of activity at Lincoln Center, contributing to an extension of the season to eleven months in which all the houses were active."[29] One was Classical Jazz, the three-concert experiment in Alice Tully Hall in August 1987 that proved so successful that it eventually evolved into Jazz at Lincoln Center, the Center's twelfth resident organization and a year-round presence on campus. The other was Serious Fun! This program of "eclectic, offbeat entertainment reflected Lincoln Center's commitment to new music and emerging artists."[30]

Management invited Jedediah Wheeler—an independent producer whose work with young, emerging artists was considered outside the mainstream—to organize and administer a seventeen-day festival of innovative, contemporary performances at Alice Tully Hall. The Fan Fox and Leslie R. Samuels Foundation provided initial support for the new series and continued to do so through the 1990 season. In 1991, the Philip Morris Companies (Altria) became the series' primary corporate funder.

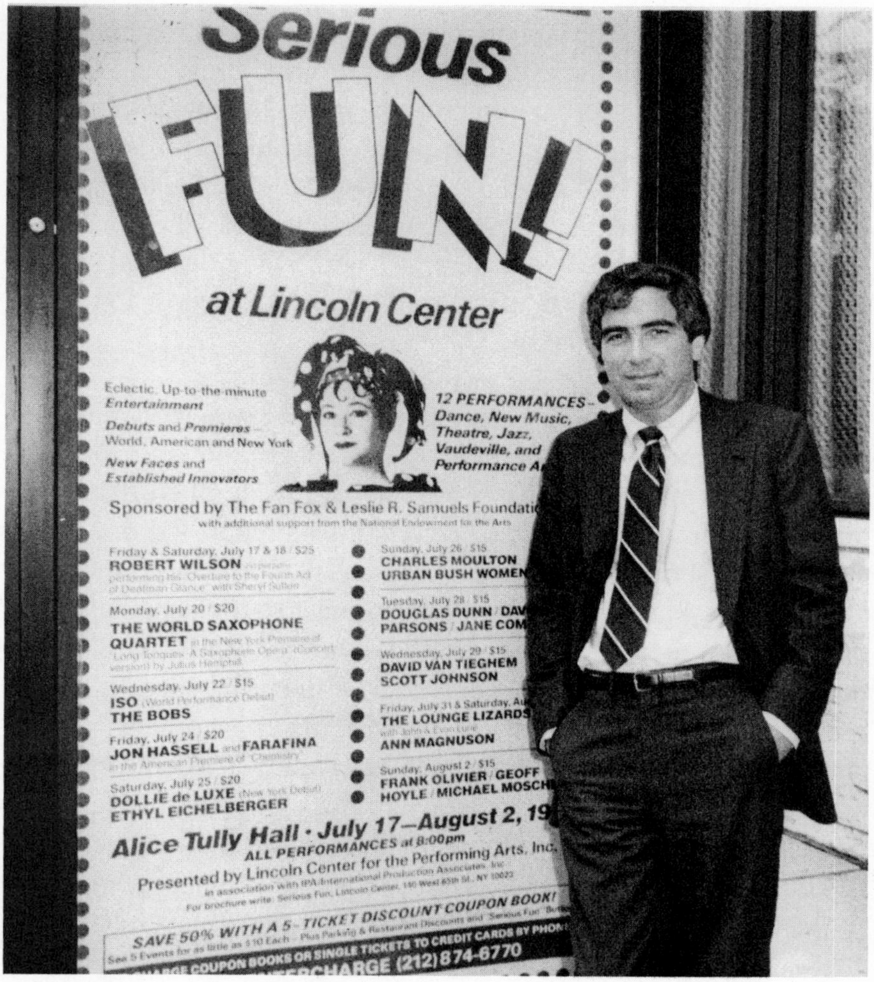

Lincoln Center president Nathan Leventhal at the opening season of Serious Fun!, 1987.

In 1987, its first summer, Serious Fun! produced more than twenty programs that "ran the gamut of contemporary performance styles from high art to low comedy."[31] Highlights included the theater artist Robert Wilson's appearance on stage in his own 1970 *Overture to the Fourth Act of Deafman Glance* and the American debut of Sarafina, Africa's premier dance-percussion group. The press embraced this effort. "Living up to both halves of its title, Serious Fun! proved to be an impressively well-rounded series integrated by aesthetics as well as by gender, race and even nationality,"[32] wrote the *Christian Science Monitor*.

Serious Fun! was so successful, in fact, that two of its presentations—Blue Man Group's *Tubes* and Bill Irwin in *Fool Moon*—later enjoyed commercial runs at other venues. And, in 1993, Serious Fun! garnered an OBIE for outstanding achievement. It firmly established Lincoln Center as a legitimate summer destination for the artistically adventuresome. It also succeeded in drawing a much younger audience to Lincoln Center and creating a sense of lively activity there.[33]

Some people still felt that New Yorkers should have an international festival of the kind William Schuman originally had envisioned. Martin E. Segal was one of them. When he became chairman of Lincoln Center in 1981, Segal expressed the hope that such an undertaking might again be considered,[34] but nothing came of the idea during his tenure.

After his retirement in 1986 as chairman, Segal set up the not-for-profit New York International Festival of the Arts and began planning the First New York International Festival of the Arts, a monthlong celebration of twentieth-century performing arts to open in June 1988. It was an ambitious undertaking, far outstripping Lincoln Center's original efforts in the late 1960s. It involved some 350 performances in music, dance, theater, symposia, multi-arts, film, and television from all over the world, presented at more than sixty locations throughout the five boroughs.[35] For the festival,

Lincoln Center agreed to coproduce, with Carnegie Hall and the New York Philharmonic, a series of orchestral concerts. In general, the press praised the effort, and Segal was pleased that "from an artistic point of view we were very successful, in that we gave a fine overview of the remarkable creations of the twentieth century."[36]

Three years later, in June 1991, the organization presented a second, scaled-down, sixteen-day festival, with performances by foreign arts companies little known to New York audiences. The press warmly praised the 1991 New York International Festival of the Arts for its artistic choices and the artistic quality of the productions. The following year, however, the organization changed course, dropping its role as producer and instead transforming itself into a vocal and effective advocate for the arts. It also became an initiator of conferences and projects that addressed the needs and opportunities of hundreds of institutions in the performing arts, a promoter of the melding of the arts and new technology, and a champion of arts education for the public schools.

Once again, New York was without a principal platform for the performing arts during the summer months. While previous efforts had demonstrated that the audiences for such an undertaking were there, what seemed to be missing was a strong institutional base that could plan, administer, and underwrite an annual international festival. Fortuitously, a number of events converged in the early 1990s that enabled Lincoln Center to undertake such a venture.

In late 1992, Jane Moss arrived at Lincoln Center, succeeding William Lockwood as executive producer and chief programmer. Moss had much to ponder as she took up her position. There was the ever-present pressure to keep the halls rented, and with terms advantageous to both Lincoln Center and its resident companies. Moss also had to deal with Mostly Mozart burnout, perhaps an inevitable result of the Center's intense, eighteen-month celebration of the Mozart bicentennial. While Mostly Mozart remained the Center's best attended and most financially stable summer program, the critics were restless. The *New York Times* critic Allan Kozinn even suggested that Lincoln Center abandon the long-running Mostly Mozart Festival, calling it "tired" and at the "end of its useful life."[37] Also, by the early 1990s, serious competition from other arts organizations, especially during the summer months, had cut into Lincoln Center's box office. Moss's mandate was to ensure that Lincoln Center maintained its competitive edge while attracting new audiences.

At the end of her first year at Lincoln Center, Moss approached management with a plan to reinvigorate the Center's summer programming. She suggested that Lincoln Center produce a world-class, multidisciplinary arts festival each July. The proposed Lincoln Center Festival would consolidate much of the Center's classical and

The Four Temperaments, the Dance Theater of Harlem, Lincoln Center Festival.

contemporary summer programming while retaining Out of Doors and Midsummer Night Swing as separate programs.[38] Moss invited all interested resident organizations to participate.

Lincoln Center chairman George Weissman and president Nathan Leventhal both enthusiastically supported Moss's idea, and the board of directors endorsed the concept, subject to the presentation of an acceptable budget. While the idea of a major festival appealed to most directors, some did express concern that it might lure donors away from individual resident organizations and have a negative effect on annual fund-raising for the Consolidated Corporate Fund, in which they all shared.

Eventually, Lincoln Center management soothed these concerns and the project moved ahead. Beverly Sills, the newly elected chairman of Lincoln Center, expressed confidence that noncompeting monies could be raised for the endeavor, which promised to be "exciting, innovative and present a nice mix of classical and contemporary."[39] In March 1995, the board approved an $8.5 million budget for the first festival—$5.5 million of which would have to be raised privately—and the newest incarnation of a summer international performing arts festival was born.

After establishing the Lincoln Center Festival as a separate department, Leventhal hired the *New York Times* music critic and cultural correspondent John Rockwell to be its director. Rockwell expressed the Center's hopes for the festival this way: "Our festival is the expression of the world's leading cultural center in the heart of the world's greatest city. We want to express the energy and diversity of New York, and epitomize its historic role as the entry port of world civilizations to the American continent and the ultimate melting pot. This festival is meant to summarize and extend what Lincoln Center has stood for over three decades: a blend of tradition and experimentation, an affirmation of quality, a model for programmatic ideas and innovations that, we hope, will have an effect far beyond the Upper West Side."[40]

Rockwell put together an interesting mix of traditional and

contemporary music and art that would occupy virtually the entire campus and a few neighboring venues as well. As the opening of Festival '96 approached with only one-third of the 85,000 tickets sold, tensions ran high. Attendance at some performances the first week was disappointing, and Lincoln Center executives held their collective breath—with an $8.5 million investment on the line. But word soon spread that something new and exciting was in the offing, and attendance picked up dramatically.

Indeed, that first festival attracted an estimated 14,000 first-timers with little or no previous experience with Lincoln Center. Robert Wilson's production of the Virgil Thomson–Gertrude Stein surrealist opera *Four Saints in Three Acts* served as the festival's centerpiece. Other highlights included all nineteen of Samuel Beckett's plays, performed by the Gate Theatre of Dublin, and the New York premiere of Merce Cunningham and John Cage's final collaboration, *Ocean*, performed in Damrosch Park. The Alvin Ailey Dance Company partnered with Wynton Marsalis and the Jazz at Lincoln Center Orchestra to perform a new work choreographed by Judith Jamison. The New York Philharmonic performed Beethoven's *Leonore* and *Fidelio* overtures in alternating performances, and the Chamber Music Society of Lincoln Center, together with the Kronos Quartet, presented the first major retrospective of the compositions of the American composer Morton Feldman.[41]

Critics praised the first festival and its mission. "In a tightly packaged twenty-one days, the theaters in and around Lincoln Center showcased a vibrant, wildly eclectic assortment of events, most of which would never have been seen here. . . . Festival '96 was a major contribution to New York's cultural life, and by the end it seemed to have entered the collective imagination of the city. Everyone was talking about it, reading about it, trying to get into the most highly touted shows."[42]

In an encouraging show of support, the Center's board authorized the continuation of the festival through 2000. And then, in the fall of 1998, with three successful seasons already under its belt, the Lincoln Center Festival became a permanent Lincoln Center program. Nigel Redden was named festival director, succeeding John Rockwell. As originally conceived, the festival had met its four primary goals: it had raised the Center's artistic profile, established the Center as a vibrant hub of cultural life in the summer, involved the Center's constituents in creative collaborations, and drawn new audiences to the campus.[43]

The summer festival had indeed fulfilled the collective hope that it would establish Lincoln Center as the venue for one of the world's

Ocean, the Merce Cunningham Dance Company performing in the Rose Theater, Lincoln Center Festival, 2005.

most prestigious performing arts festivals. It continues to attract unusual offerings that would otherwise not be seen in the United States, such as the celebrated Chinese opera *The Peony Pavilion* in 1999, or a trio of Iranian passion plays, *Ta'zieh*, as well as special homegrown offerings, such as the 2005 revival of Merce Cunningham's marvelous *Ocean*, a dance piece with music by John Cage that was presented at Lincoln Center's first festival, in 1996.

The Peony Pavilion, Chinese opera, Lincoln Center Festival, 1999.

American Songbook

In the summer of 1996, with Jazz at Lincoln Center firmly established as the Center's twelfth resident organization and the Lincoln Center Festival successfully launched, Center programmers considered additional ways to fill gaps in programming to attract new audiences. A 1996 study, "Lincoln Center Programming Options," suggested the need for "a greater spirit of innovation" to reinvigorate Lincoln Center's sagging Great Performers series.[44] Over the next few years, this was successfully accomplished (and is chronicled earlier in this chapter). At the same time, management turned its attention to developing American Songbook, a new series that would showcase the popular song, or "standard," sometimes referred to as "American classical music."

. . .

American Songbook premiered in 1999. The idea for it began with Lincoln Center president Nathan Leventhal, a fan of that genre since boyhood. It became his pet project, and he shepherded the program through a difficult first year to enjoy critical and popular acclaim the next. Leventhal remembered, "My thought was we could perpetuate this music—the great American standards of our century."[45]

When first presented with the idea of Lincoln Center sponsoring a series on popular music of the twentieth century, its directors engaged in a lengthy and animated discussion. A few expressed the often-voiced concern that the Center would be broadening its role as a producer and thus competing with the resident companies for audiences and ultimately for funds. In the end, however, management moved ahead.[46]

Leventhal and Jane Moss invited Jonathan Schwartz, a New York disc jockey and a well-known connoisseur of the popular song, to serve as an artistic consultant. "Schwartz was a shrewd choice," said the *New York Times*, "because he is well-connected to both classic pop audiences and performers alike. He has also been a fanatical crusader for the American popular song."[47] Schwartz poetically defined a standard as "a popular song experienced generationally in the ongoing editorial process of life, so that its fragrance hovers potently above all that is temporary. A standard is a carefully crafted vessel of feelings that sails into the soul and remains forever."[48]

The series' first season offered two sets of programs in Alice Tully Hall: one featuring the songs of the late Harold Arlen and the other devoted to the late Richard Rodgers. "When tickets went on sale for the first four shows of the American Songbook in February and March at Alice Tully Hall, they were sold out in a matter of hours. . . . The instant demand for the American Songbook series suggests that the market for traditional pop is larger and hungrier than many like to imagine,"[49] said the *New York Times*. Yet American Songbook experienced a rocky start, as the Arlen program suffered technical and acoustical difficulties that did not go unnoticed by the

Audra McDonald in *I Gotta Right to Sing the Blues: The Music of Harold Arlen*, on the opening night of American Songbook, February 5, 1999.

New York press. By the time the Rodgers program opened the following month, however, American Songbook had settled in.

American Songbook strongly appealed to audiences and critics alike. "If the series can do for traditional pop what Jazz at Lincoln Center has done for jazz," one critic wrote, "Lincoln Center's commitment to American popular song could be an enormous boost to the genre that was eclipsed at mid-century by Elvis Presley and rock-and-roll."[50]

The following fall, American Songbook found its sea legs, producing well-received programs of songs by Jimmy Van Heusen and Jerome Kern. Later, a cabaret component was added. "Just like with Jazz for the first few years, we're experimenting with different formats. It's getting better and better, but we're still feeling our way,"

Leventhal said in 2000.[51] Soon, songs of living composers were added to appeal to younger audiences.

Schwartz departed after the 2000–2001 season. Eventually, American Songbook's presentations were relocated from the 1,000-seat Alice Tully Hall to the smaller and more intimate Stanley H. Kaplan Penthouse, a venue more conducive to cabaret-type performances. With the opening of Jazz at Lincoln Center's facilities in late 2004 in the Time Warner Center, an expanded and reconceived American Songbook again relocated. Most of its performances are now presented in Jazz at Lincoln Center's new Allen Room, which accommodates between three hundred and six hundred people. In its 2005–2006 season, it enjoyed a record-breaking box office. "It has made an impact on the New York cultural map," Jane Moss told the board, "due to the diversification of its programming beyond popular standards and by the decision to present most performances in the Jazz at Lincoln Center complex."[52]

Live from Lincoln Center

On the evening of January 30, 1976, André Previn strode to the podium in Philharmonic Hall, acknowledged the audience's applause, nodded at the guest soloist Van Cliburn, and, as the first notes of Grieg's Piano Concerto floated through the air, inaugurated the first of many years of live, televised performances from Lincoln Center. John O'Keefe, the Center's vice president for public information, later noted the powerful impact of this single event: "It wasn't until we went on the air that night with Van Cliburn and the New York Philharmonic that all of a sudden the world understood what Lincoln Center was."[53]

Live from Lincoln Center has been one of the institution's most successful initiatives over the past thirty years. Featuring performances presented both by its own resident companies and by Lincoln Center, Inc., the series has, in fact, as O'Keefe observed, "opened everything up—the fund-raising, the media attention, the acceptance of the arts."[54]

From the beginning, Lincoln Center's leaders understood that the new communications technology might hold a vast potential for their project. Television had an insatiable appetite for content, and all three major networks, following the example of radio in the 1920s and 1930s, had broadcast live classical music and other performing arts during prime time—although situation comedies, sports, and variety shows dominated even during the early years of the medium. CBS had presented *Omnibus* and the Philharmonic's *Young People's Concerts* with Leonard Bernstein conducting. (In fact, TV turned the charismatic Bernstein into a popular icon and celebrity.) As a result, Lincoln Center's performance halls had been built to accommodate television equipment, and CBS televised the Philharmonic's opening concert in 1962. Before the invention of videotape, all these television programs were necessarily live.

Much had been done during Lincoln Center's first ten years, but it seemed that even more might be achieved in the future. To explore the full potential of television programming, the Center's management turned to John Goberman. A cellist turned media consultant, Goberman had been involved in a 1971 experiment in which two local cable outlets televised live the New York City Opera's production of *Le Coq d'Or* from the New York State Theater. The broadcast drew a respectable audience, and Goberman sought to interest Lincoln Center in doing more live shows. Carlos Moseley, the Philharmonic's manager, was intrigued and introduced Goberman to Lincoln Center chairman Amyas Ames and to John O'Keefe, the vice president for public information.

John Goberman, Lincoln Center's director of media development and the mastermind behind *Live from Lincoln Center*.

They were impressed and soon asked Goberman to head a media-development effort for Lincoln Center.

Goberman set up the Media Department in 1972 and quickly developed a strategy to exploit the possibilities of television for Lincoln Center. At the same time, he experimented with taping performances by the Center's resident companies, starting with the New York City Ballet's performance of *Jewels*. Almost immediately, Goberman realized that successful live broadcasts would require negotiations with the various unions for the right to make reference tapes of rehearsals and performances in order to prepare for the actual live broadcast.

His effort was greatly aided by a series of annual Sloan Foundation grants, which began in 1973, to solve the technical problems inherent in transmitting live performances effectively. Other contributors, including the Ford Foundation and the John and Mary R. Markle Foundation, joined in this effort. These grants assisted in the development of cameras capable of functioning in low stage light and also made possible stereo simulcasts on radio.

Goberman and his associates refined the strategic approach to television. From the beginning Goberman, Ames, and Center president John Mazzola envisioned a separate subscription arts channel for Lincoln Center. The advent of cable had stimulated interest in creating dedicated cable channels just for the performing arts. After much trial and effort, though, the commercial companies decided that a channel based on subscriptions was not feasible, and they opted for advertiser-supported approaches. This would lead eventually to cable channels such as the Arts & Entertainment Network.

Finally, in 1975, Goberman, Ames, and Mazzola began to discuss airing live Lincoln Center performances on public television. They all saw this option as the bridge to their goal of a subscription pay channel. There was lively discussion of the wisdom of such an interim step. Indeed, as late as October 1975, Robert Kreidler, the president of the Sloan Foundation, expressed deep pessimism. "While I have not the slightest doubt that actual telecasting of a 'live' series from Lincoln Center would help 'build a market' in the short run, I worry that it might seriously jeopardize your long-range objective. As my colleague Steve White put it: 'If you begin by giving it away, how will you hope ever to sell it?'"[55]

While these doubts persisted, Lincoln Center concluded that the only real possibility was a *Live from Lincoln Center* series on public television. In the spring of 1975, the Center began conversations about support for the project with Stephen Stamas, the vice president for public affairs at Exxon Corporation, and other Exxon officials.

In mid-June, Ames and Mazzola, along with Jay Iselin, the president of WNET/13, met with Exxon's representatives, led by Stamas, who indicated a willingness to underwrite a substantial part of the three-year *Live from Lincoln Center* project. They planned six broadcasts for 1976 and contemplated ten live performances in 1977 and twelve in 1978. The three-year budget was $5 million, and Exxon was prepared to put up $1 million in the first year on condition that the rest of the money could be raised.

Lincoln Center informed Exxon and WNET/13 that the Metropolitan Opera would not be included in the project because of the possibility that the Met would be sponsored separately on television by its longtime radio sponsor, Texaco. It was agreed, however, to include the Met in the series as a seventh presentation of *Live from Lincoln Center* in 1976 if these plans changed.

The Metropolitan Opera's management was clearly relieved that the conflict of sponsorship between Exxon and Texaco made it easy for the Met to stay out of *Live from Lincoln Center*. There was some feeling at the Met that participation might lead to loss of artistic control.[56] The Met has proceeded with its own series—the performances at first presented live but soon thereafter taped for later transmission—significantly increasing Lincoln Center's reach beyond its concert halls.

John Goberman and the Lincoln Center management faced a different kind of challenge in persuading the New York City Ballet to participate in *Live from Lincoln Center*. Even though one of the first experimental tapes had been a performance of the ballet *Jewels*, both the artistic director George Balanchine and the general director Lincoln Kirstein had reservations about television. Kirstein worried about who would control the cameras and also thought the home TV screen was too small to accommodate a large number of dancers.[57] In a similar vein, John Mazzola recalled Balanchine saying, "You have ants, little ants. Big screen, little ants."[58]

Two events probably helped Lincoln Center bring the New York City Ballet into the fold. One was the highly successful *Live from Lincoln Center* presentation in June 1977 of the American Ballet Theatre's *Giselle*, which attracted the largest audience by far of the new series.[59] The second development was Balanchine's agreement to participate in a four-part presentation of his ballets on the "Dance in America" portion of public television's *Great Performances* program. Balanchine personally supervised the videotaping of these programs in Nashville, Tennessee, and choreographed anew some parts to make them more compatible with the camera.

The experience seems to have assuaged the master's fears. Even as he was planning the Nashville tapings, Balanchine agreed to participate in *Live from Lincoln Center*. In January 1978, the New York City Ballet presented *Coppelia* to great acclaim, winning an Emmy, television's highest award for excellence.

Even with this early success, the Ballet's ambivalence about television did not totally disappear. After the successful *Coppelia* and despite Balanchine's involvement with the "Dance in America" series, his company did not appear again on *Live from Lincoln Center* until October 1982, with a special program honoring the historic collaboration between Stravinsky and Balanchine. Then, in May 1986, the company presented Balanchine's choreography of *A Midsummer Night's Dream*, followed by a live television program in 1989 with Ray Charles. A new version of *Swan Lake*, choreographed by Peter Martins, was televised in 1999, in connection with the fiftieth anniversary of the company. The New York City Ballet's most recent appearance on *Live from Lincoln Center* came in 2004 with its homage to its founder George Balanchine on the hundredth anniversary of his birth.

From its inception, *Live from Lincoln Center* planned to include theater in its mix of programming. In 1987, Lincoln Center Theater presented a daring production of Shakespeare's *The Comedy of Errors* as interpreted by the Flying Karamazov Brothers, which garnered mixed reactions and results. Goberman and Kirk Browning, who directed most of the *Live from Lincoln Center* productions, concluded that a live theater production did not translate well to the television screen because of special technical problems. Notwithstanding the long and honorable history of live drama on television (before the availability of tape), specially prepared and taped studio versions of plays had prevailed for years.

To finance *Live from Lincoln Center*, Stephen Stamas persuaded Exxon to cover half the cost of six productions a year, and the National Endowment for the Arts and the Corporation for Public Broadcasting provided the balance. This pattern (with some additional funding for special purposes) continued until Exxon's withdrawal in 1989. In 1987, the Robert Wood Johnson, Jr. Charitable Trust joined as an underwriter and remained one. George Weissman was helpful in securing General Motors to replace Exxon as the major corporate underwriter of the program, which it continued through 1993. After a hiatus of four years, during which the Lila Wallace–Reader's Digest Fund covered a substantial share of the cost, MetLife signed on as the major corporate sponsor.

The Lila Wallace–Reader's Digest Fund also provided funding for a feature that accompanied the live telecasts—*Backstage\Lincoln Center*. This lively and imaginative intermission program helped viewers better understand what they were seeing. From its beginning, critics and audiences praised *Backstage*, and its intermission clips were often used as stand-alone resources for its educational programs.

Intermission features had been a part of *Live from Lincoln Center* from the very first program, which Carlos Moseley hosted. Over the years, several distinguished individuals took the chair during intermission, including Hugh Downs, who brought to the role the luster of his commercial television career, along with his passion and obvious commitment to the performing arts. Other well-known hosts included Garrick Utley, Dick Cavett, Robert McNeil, Gene Shalit, Patrick Watson, and Beverly Sills.

John Goberman intended *Backstage* to supplement the live telecasts with a useful educational component. The first program, in January 1994, included interviews with Andre Watts, Luciano Pavarotti, and other leading artists. Critics and viewers appreciated the program's high standards, and it was a considerable disappointment to all when funding could not be sustained after 1998, following the withdrawal of the Lila Wallace–Reader's Digest Fund. As good as the standard intermission interviews were, the loss of *Backstage* was regrettable.

The year 1998 was also critical for the funding of *Live from Lincoln Center*. While MetLife had come in as a corporate sponsor, the rising costs of the series required Lincoln Center's management to reach out to other sources. For the 2000 fiscal year, in addition to MetLife, funders included the Robert Wood Johnson, Jr. Charitable Trust; the Fan Fox and Leslie R. Samuels Foundation; Thomas H. Lee and Ann Tenenbaum; and Mr. and Mrs. Frederick P. Rose.

The costs of producing six telecasts a year have never been officially released, but outside observers estimated the average annual total at $3 million. From the beginning, John Goberman and Lincoln Center wisely included a fee for participation by a resident organization in a telecast, but the bulk of the costs were related to production, artist fees, and transmission. While satellite transmission costs have decreased over the years, there have been no significant breakthroughs in reducing the technical costs of television productions and transmission.

Live from Lincoln Center has provided a remarkable variety of performing-arts programs for nearly thirty years. One of its early memorable evenings featured Luciano Pavarotti in recital at the Metropolitan Opera House in February 1978. Pavarotti has often credited this and subsequent appearances on *Live from Lincoln Center* and *Live from the Met* as major influences in his popularity and star status.

The New York Philharmonic, first under the maestro Zubin Mehta and then under Kurt Masur and Lorin Maazel, has usually participated in two programs each year. Its contributions have included collaborations with some of the most celebrated artists of

Tenor Luciano Pavarotti in concert as part of the Great Performers series, televised on *Live from Lincoln Center* on February 2, 1978.

Live from Lincoln Center rehearsal for the New York Philharmonic's opening night, September 16, 1986. Seated: Maestro Zubin Mehta (left) with John Goberman, Lincoln Center's director of media development.

the day—Rudolf Serkin, Itzhak Perlman, Placido Domingo, Yo-Yo Ma, and Jessye Norman. The New York City Opera has also been well represented on *Live from Lincoln Center*, making available over the years not only the standard and well-known operas *La Bohème* and *La Traviata* but also Leos Janáček's *The Cunning Little Vixen* and Benjamin Britton's *Paul Bunyan*.

John Goberman's guiding principle for *Live from Lincoln Center* was to present the full spectrum of the performing arts as they existed at Lincoln Center. He accomplished this goal in large measure. As early as 1978, he telecast a program by the Chamber Music Society of Lincoln Center to critical approval, dispelling doubts about the appeal of chamber music on television. The Chamber Music Society has been a regular participant ever since. In 1985,

Live from Lincoln Center first televised the season's opening Mostly Mozart concert, which it continued to do for most subsequent seasons. Telecasts originated from Juilliard on its eightieth anniversary, as well as from the Film Society, the Great Performers series, the Lincoln Center Festival, Jazz at Lincoln Center, and, in 1998, Lincoln Center Theater's *Twelfth Night*. American Ballet Theatre, which is not a constituent of Lincoln Center but performs regularly in the Metropolitan Opera House, was well represented in the early years.

In 1989, John Goberman and the Lincoln Center management experimented with wider distribution of some of the *Live from Lincoln Center* telecasts. Nine videocassettes were produced to test the market. Although the project covered its costs, it became clear to Goberman that the supply of older and current performing arts productions had overwhelmed demand and that the potential market for *Live from Lincoln Center* videocassettes was limited. No further releases were made; however, Lincoln Center has been careful to preserve its legal position in regard to its library of *Live from Lincoln Center* programs. Goberman and his colleagues have continued to examine prospects for wider distribution beyond the live telecasts, especially in light of rapid technological changes. It is known that any progress in this area would also have to deal with artist clearances for uses beyond the original telecasts.

How does one assess the success and the impact of *Live from Lincoln Center*? The program clearly extended the reach and the visibility of the performing arts. Although television audience ratings vary by program, the series has sustained a large public television viewership throughout its history. The evidence includes the continued willingness of public television stations to pay a share of the costs through PBS's complicated bidding process each year. One has only to recall that public television executives openly questioned the attractiveness of classical music telecasts as late as the mid-1970s. While there are too few other performing arts telecasts available on public television and even fewer live programs, *Live from Lincoln Center* has helped to establish a demand for such programming.

No other cultural center has been able to emulate Lincoln Center in providing regular live telecasts of its activities. The costs of such productions remain high, and artist-clearance problems and other obstacles remain—including the limited financial resources of performing arts organizations and of public television itself.

The original dream of a separate pay subscription channel has not been achieved and still seems far away, but this is not because Lincoln Center has neglected technological and market possibilities. Whenever a potential market outlet has appeared, Lincoln Center has been well placed to explore it.

The impact of public television on Lincoln Center itself has been enormous. It has projected the constituent companies to a broader public than ever before possible. As an example, each New York Philharmonic telecast reaches millions more people than the 300,000 individuals who come to hear the Philharmonic during a whole season. And there is clear evidence that the telecasts have stimulated interest in music, dance, and the other performing arts represented on *Live from Lincoln Center*. The initial concern of some that the programs would reduce ticket sales has proved unwarranted; the contrary has occurred. Lincoln Center has achieved its iconic status primarily because of the artistic excellence on its stages, but there is little doubt that television has also played an important part. The visibility of Lincoln Center and its constituent companies has assisted fund-raising and volunteer participation, as well as audience development.

High costs and limits to what can be raised to support telecasts have curtailed the public television series to six or seven programs each year, instead of the ten or more originally envisioned. Yet when one looks back on what has been achieved since the first telecast in 1976, one can only conclude that *Live from Lincoln Center* has been one of the most successful and important television initiatives of the last thirty years.

Community Programming

Leonard de Paur, Lincoln Center's first director of community relations, 1972.

"I remember being up in the Philharmonic's offices one day," recalled the late Leonard de Paur, who was hired in 1970 as Lincoln Center's first director of community relations. "I looked out the window. Here was this magnificent plaza and not a thing on it but pigeons. I thought of some of the places I had seen in Europe, and I said, 'What a shame. It's gorgeous, it's beautiful, it's wonderful, and nobody is making any use of it or deriving any benefit from it.' Lincoln Center is a home of the living arts, and by God, if we can't bring some life in here, we're not fulfilling our mandate."[60]

Bring the community to Lincoln Center and take Lincoln Center to the community, management told de Paur.[61] The times are turbulent, and the Center must respond!

De Paur and his colleagues immediately went to work, devising an approach that would eventually blossom into a series of innovative programs that strengthened and deepened the Center's commitment to its immediate neighborhoods and the community at large. In the process, the great fountain plaza and other outdoor areas of Lincoln Center came alive in the way de Paur had dreamed they would.

The social and racial upheavals of the 1960s had cut an angry swath through America's urban centers. Riots in Watts, Detroit, Newark, and many other cities, large and small, had revealed the festering discontent and profound alienation of many of the country's poor and minority citizens. Out of this turmoil and agitation evolved a unique brand of art called "street theater." The plays and other kinds of productions written and performed by residents of those troubled communities portrayed their own lives, quite often in brutal and profane ways. It was "theater of, for, and by the people," very different from the Center's usual offerings and often compelling. The energy and the emotion of it could not be ignored.

In 1971, Geraldine Fitzgerald, the Irish-born actress and cofounder of Everyman Theater, approached Lincoln Center management with a proposal for a ten-day summer festival featuring twelve street theater groups from neighborhoods in New York City, Washington, Los Angeles, and San Francisco. While the groups would perform in all five boroughs, she wanted to use Lincoln Center as the festival's principal platform. Amyas Ames, the chairman of Lincoln Center, and John Mazzola, the executive vice president and chief operating officer, saw the importance that Fitzgerald's proposal could have for the Center and agreed to cooperate. They created the Department of Community Affairs and appointed Leonard de Paur director. An energetic man with strong ties to New York's black community, de Paur set to work immediately to plan the opening festivities.

The result of the collaboration between Lincoln Center and Fitzgerald's group was the first annual Everyman-Community Street Theater Festival, held August 19–29, 1971. More than 800 people performed, including 250 New York City schoolchildren, and they used every possible space as a stage, including the balconies of every building. "All the performers were amateurs. . . . Their concentration and dedication were more than just touching and their flashes of talent . . . impressive," wrote Edith Oliver in the *New Yorker*.[62] Local restaurants provided free box lunches, and there were plenty of soft drinks, too.

The press enthusiastically embraced the event. "Playing for audiences on the steps of the Juilliard School and around the fountain on the beautiful open plaza, the twelve groups filled the air with exuberance, pride, frustration and anger, and left a density of theatrical feeling that was a revelation to many who had come to be entertained," noted *Newsweek* magazine.[63] "Behind the blue banner proclaiming Everyman-Community Street Theater Festival at Lincoln Center, the plaza teemed with sound, color and humanity yesterday at noon," the *New York Times* critic Howard Thompson reported about the opening-day festivities. "Several thousand people thronged the vast mall, dotted with colorful balloons and food carts and throbbing with the beat of bongo drums and electronic rhythm bands."[64]

The festival was such a success that de Paur, with management's backing, began to plan a second festival for the following summer. In addition, the Center agreed to host a Community Holiday Festival for a two-week, ten-performance program beginning December 22, 1971. "Lincoln Center for the Performing Arts, the citadel of the American cultural Establishment, announced yesterday that for the first time it is opening its doors to neighborhood performing artists,"[65] proclaimed the *New York Times*. While not altogether accurate, the story did recognize that Lincoln Center had embarked on a new course by reaching out to communities that might be unfamiliar with ballet, opera, and classical music. Con Edison and the City of New York provided financial and logistical assistance, and the Center assembled a diverse array of dancers, singers, musicians, and actors from Harlem, Chinatown, Queens, Brooklyn, and the Bronx in Alice Tully Hall that December.

Vitrine advertising Lincoln Center's Community Holiday Festival, 1990.

The press appreciated that the Community Holiday Festival was part of the Center's broader effort to include a wider spectrum of New Yorkers in its activities. "Lincoln Center is moving out to people in exactly the right way by bringing them from all walks of life right into the Center itself. Culture isn't buildings, but a handsome setting enhances both the [food] carts and those who come to share in their magic."[66]

The following year, the Center presented Soul at the Center, produced by Ellis Haizlip—a celebration of the black experience in the performing arts, with encores in 1973 and 1974. It was programming "sought by and aided by that mighty fortress and port in the storm of ancient European music, Lincoln Center," wrote Carman Moore in the *Saturday Review*. Moore lauded the effort and noted that "the hopes both of the soul and the Center seem to have been so well realized. . . . With halls at least two-thirds filled and with audiences that looked to me two-thirds black . . . the very first blush of a new friendship seems possible."[67]

The Community Holiday Festival ran for twenty-three successful seasons and left Lincoln Center an enduring legacy of artistic achievement and community involvement. It encouraged and guided new talent, cultivated new audiences, and strengthened Lincoln Center's ties with its neighbors.[68]

By the early 1990s, the format had grown a bit stale, however, and in 1993 Lincoln Center reorganized its community outreach effort, which resulted in an eclectic mix of programs that included Young Musicmakers, featuring concert bands, choirs, jazz, and other musical ensembles from school, university, and community groups throughout the country, performing on the Josie Robertson Plaza; art exhibitions in the Center's Cork Gallery on the concourse level of Avery Fisher Hall; an audience development program that selectively distributes free or discounted tickets to performances to a variety of community and nonprofit organizations; the annual Christmas-tree lighting on the plaza; and the twice-yearly American Craft Festival on the plaza.

Lincoln Center Out of Doors, the Center's signature summer programming effort, was established in 1974. It built on the success of the earlier Everyman-Community Street Theater Festival, which,

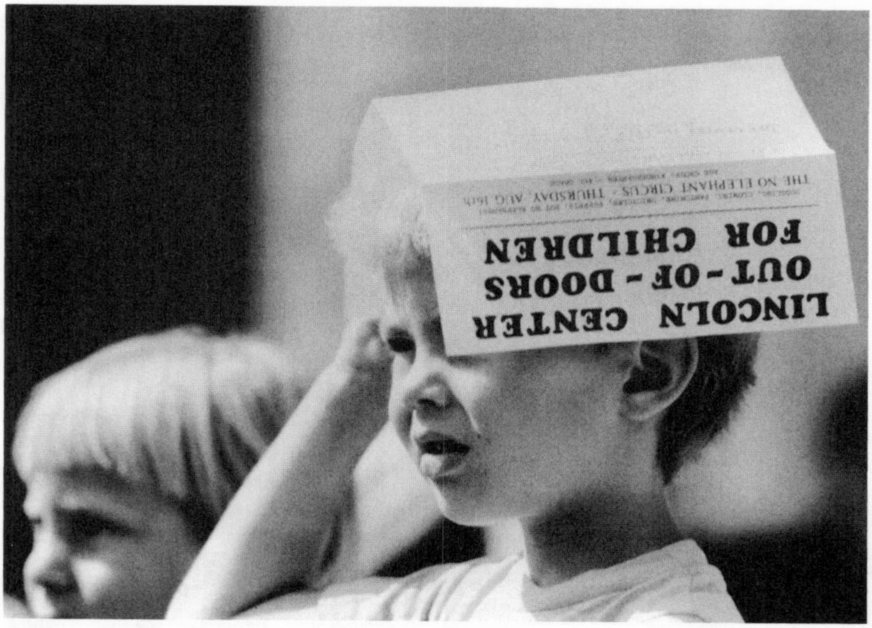

Lincoln Center Out of Doors for Children, 1984.

with its heavy emphasis on provocative street theater performed by amateurs, had become outdated and underattended. Yet the basic idea behind the festival—staging performances on the plaza open to the broadest possible public—was still valid.

Out of Doors began as a two-week festival of fifty free performances—street theater, dance, musical comedy, chamber music, symphony, and jazz—on the plaza and in Damrosch Park. Facing its own budgetary woes at the time, Lincoln Center sought outside funding for the program and found it with the Exxon Corporation.[69] Out of Doors featured some of the country's finest black and Hispanic performing artists and groups and actively reached out to audiences from those communities.

From its inception, critics and audiences alike reacted warmly to Out of Doors. The festival continued to expand in size and scope and served as a venue through which jazz and modern dance were presented at Lincoln Center. It thrived "as one of the largest free

The Spanish Teatro Guirigai at Lincoln Center Out of Doors, August 2003.

public performing-arts events in the country. Each summer, Out of Doors made accessible," the *New York Times* wrote, "the highest caliber of dance music and performance artistry from around the globe to over 200,000 visitors."[70] It became a viable forum for artists and artistic collaborations with other institutions, according to Jenneth Webster, currently associate director of programming. "Arts change the way people look at the world for a while and give them a glorious exposure."[71]

In 1989, Katherine O'Neill, at that time the director of special projects, went to chairman George Weissman and the Lincoln Center management with a proposal for how to celebrate the Center's thirtieth anniversary: invite the public to "twenty glorious nights of dancing under the stars" on the plaza. Weissman and the board approved the plan, and, with Citibank's support, Lincoln Center invited big bands and steel bands, jazz bands and Dixieland bands, samba and salsa to take over the plaza. The program was an instant, huge hit. Everything sold out. And so Lincoln Center found itself with another successful summer series, which it called Midsummer Night Swing.

Within a few years, those in attendance could take dance lessons as well as listen to zydeco, merengue, and hip-hop. Dessert Night—featuring sweets from a number of Manhattan restaurants—was

Crowds gather to enjoy Midsummer Night Swing on the Josie Robertson Plaza.

added as a special fund-raiser in 1994, the same year Daisy and Paul Soros and the William H. Kearns Foundation took over sponsorship. By 1998, Midsummer Night Swing had become a five-week summer delight. "When it's dark out, the sight of every house at intermission—the intermissions sometimes coincide, and everybody's on the terraces looking down at the swirl of dancers, the bright lights and the dancing—it's one of the great sights of New York."[72]

Children's Programming

Lincoln Center has always devoted a generous portion of its energies to children's programming and to developing collaborative programs that deepen their understanding of, and appreciation for, the performing arts. The Center's founders discussed this issue, and it was an explicit part of John D. Rockefeller 3rd's vision that Lincoln Center make the performing arts available to all.

Some resident organizations had ongoing educational programs for schoolchildren that predated their moves to Lincoln Center in the 1960s. At Lincoln Center, they sponsored family-friendly programs, such as the Philharmonic's Young People's Concerts, or seasonal performances of repertory pieces, such as the New York City Ballet's *The Nutcracker* and the Metropolitan Opera's *Hansel and Gretel*. There were also programs crafted especially for children, such as the Film Society of Lincoln Center's Movies for Kids—which ran for ten years, until 2001, when its major funding was withdrawn—or Jazz at Lincoln Center's Jazz for Young People concert series. Many of these programs and performances were made available at substantially reduced rates to encourage participation. In addition, outside groups presented children's programming on the Lincoln Center campus. For example, the Little Orchestra Society, under the maestro Dino Anagnost, regularly gave concerts for children in Avery Fisher Hall. And, in 1977, the Big Apple Circus set up its tent in Damrosch Park and has continued to do so ever since.

. . .

Lincoln Center's own efforts to create and produce meaningful children's programming have taken several forms. (The Lincoln Center Institute, its most extensive effort in the area of education, is chronicled in the following section of this chapter.) Special events for children were consistently incorporated in three of Lincoln Center's ongoing programs: Out of Doors, Midsummer Night Swing, and the Lincoln Center Festival. On occasion, the Center also offered series developed especially for young people, such as the Introducing Lincoln Center family sampler series in the late 1980s, which featured weekend main-stage matinee performances by the New York City Ballet, the New York City Opera, the New York Philharmonic, and the Metropolitan Opera, all geared to children six years of age and older, and their families.[73] Beginning in April 2000, the Center's Passport to the World of Performing Arts program, established in 1985, broadened its offerings, as its information sheet explains, to give children of "different backgrounds and abilities the opportunity to experience the magic of live performances" and participate in "multidisciplinary arts education programs at Lincoln Center throughout the school year." In 2004, Great Performers added its first interactive family series, Family Musik, with the composer and conductor Robert Kapilow.

Three programs, however, illustrate the ways in which Lincoln Center, Inc., has continued over the years to broaden and enrich its children's programming: the Meet-the-Artist School Series, the Celebration Series, and Reel to Real.

Instituted by the Department of Visitor Services in 1975 to supplement its one-hour tours for adults of the Metropolitan Opera House, Avery Fisher Hall, and the New York State Theater, Meet-the-Artist offered visitors the opportunity for face-to-face conversational encounters with Lincoln Center's onstage and backstage artists—singers, dancers, conductors, actors, instrumentalists, designers, choreographers—from the resident companies.[74] The program soon expanded to include artists not directly associated with Lincoln Center.[75]

In 1979, Meet-the-Artist branched out to offer metropolitan area schools the opportunity to bring students in grades 3 through 12 to Lincoln Center for an inside look at what the performing arts are all about.[76] After a brief tour of Lincoln Center, students met with participating artists to explore ideas and ask questions. In 1981, this new effort became a formal Meet-the-Artist School Series. The following year, a performance element, featuring theater, opera, mime, clowning, and dance performances, was added to enhance the program's conversational element. At that time, some fourteen hundred children participated each year in the program.

In April 2000, the Meet-the-Artist School Series extended its work to children with disabilities through Lincoln Center's Passport to the World of Performing Arts program. Passport also provided opportunities throughout the school year for children with disabilities to engage in multidisciplinary arts-education programs at the Center, including fully underwritten performance tickets and hands-on arts workshops.[77]

By 2005, the Meet-the-Artist School Series was staging more than a hundred performances a year for more than fifteen thousand school-age children, including nearly two thousand children with disabilities, from approximately three hundred public and private schools in the New York metropolitan area. In commenting upon the success of the program, Alina Bloomgarden, the former head of Visitor Services at Lincoln Center, explained, "There is nothing more fascinating than someone's story. And that's exactly what Meet-the-Artist is all about. There's something about that which is endlessly interesting. The artists love telling their story, and people love drawing it out of them."[78]

When Alina Bloomgarden arrived at Lincoln Center in 1981 to head Visitor Services, she wanted to see Lincoln Center expand its children's programming. She approached Center chairman Martin E. Segal about joining forces with the famed ballet dancer Jacques

Jacques d'Amboise (center, rear), former principal dancer with the New York City Ballet, with his own National Dance Institute's dancers, May 1986.

d'Amboise and his National Dance Institute, which d'Amboise had created in 1976 to encourage children's lifelong involvement in the arts through the medium of dance.[79] Segal readily and enthusiastically agreed.

Celebration Series, a coproduction of Lincoln Center's Meet-the-Artist program and the National Dance Institute, premiered in November 1985, offering full-scale original musical productions with children and well-known actors, actresses, dancers, and singers performing together. The National Dance Institute withdrew as coproducer after four seasons in order to expand its own successful arts-education program in the public schools. Lincoln Center continued to produce the Celebration Series on its own through 1993. Its very last performance, *Claire's Broom Detective Agency: The Mystery of the Missing Violin*, featured the violinist Itzhak Perlman, who described the effort as "a wonderful opportunity for young people to become involved with music, dance, and drama, either as a performer or as a member of the audience."[80]

Reel to Real, a collaboration of Lincoln Center, Inc., and the Film Society of Lincoln Center, debuted in 1996. It combined film, live programming, and audience participation and was enthusiastically received not only by its young audience but by their parents as well. Each season, eight different weekend programs were presented. Reel to Real mixed "the appeal of Meet-the-Artist programming, with its simple production values featuring direct contact with artists as both performers and personalities, and a Saturday-at-the-movies film experience for children and families."[81] In 2000, Lincoln Center took Reel to Real on the road for the first time, to the New York metropolitan region and later beyond.

Lincoln Center Institute for the Arts in Education

> To teach values found in all kinds of genuine creativity; expressiveness, clarity, warmth, persuasiveness, emotional power, unity, consistency—these are qualities to be found everywhere in art and in many different kinds of artistic expression. The ability to recognize these values in the essence of aesthetic perception should be the first goal of all education programs in the arts.[82]
>
> —MARK SCHUBART, ON THE OCCASION OF LINCOLN CENTER INSTITUTE'S TWENTY-FIFTH ANNIVERSARY, 2001

By the standards of the time, Lincoln Center's initial efforts in the early 1960s at bringing the performing arts to metropolitan area elementary and secondary schoolchildren were laudable. High on its founders' list of goals for the Center was the establishment of an active education component, to be administered by a separate department, that would "provide opportunities for large numbers of young people to be exposed to the enjoyment of all the performing arts."[83] Mark Schubart, the former dean and vice president of the Juilliard School, arrived at Lincoln Center in 1963 to spearhead the effort, known as the Lincoln Center Student Program.

"In the early days of the Center," Schubart once explained to a journalist, "we settled on the now-traditional approach of bringing performing groups into the schools and bringing students to performances at the Center. The assumption then was that if children were exposed to the arts, they would respond automatically."[84] Three Lincoln Center resident organizations—the Metropolitan Opera, the New York Philharmonic, and the Juilliard School—already operated educational programs, which had been put in place long before they joined the Lincoln Center federation. Their efforts included special matinee performances for high school students from the New York area and touring programs. Schubart worked to include other members of the Lincoln Center family in a similar effort, which essentially relied on this kind of "passive" exposure to stimulate developing interest in the performing arts.

By its tenth year, the Center's educational program had reached nearly six million students.[85] Yet Schubart, increasingly troubled by what he saw as the program's inability to touch young people, began to think about arts education in a different way. "All we were doing was educating kids to love Lincoln Center, but that was really labor bringing forth a mouse—so gigantic an enterprise really deserved a more significant role."[86] Schubart secured a grant from the Carnegie Corporation and spent a year puzzling through the issues surrounding the central question of whether the arts were an important component of education.

In 1972, Schubart published his conclusions in the study *The Hunting of the Squiggle*, findings so noteworthy that they made the front page of the *New York Times*.[87] Essentially, he determined that traditional arts-education programs acted primarily as audience-development efforts and were not genuinely educational. He called for radical change. Instead of the typical "presentation of recognized works in a formal setting, which now makes up the bulk of what passes for youth programs," there should be "smaller, informal projects involving artists, which would attempt to form basic aesthetic perceptions in the young."[88] To achieve this, Schubart championed the establishment of an institution—not merely a program—where artists, educators, parents, and children could join together in a process of interdisciplinary collaboration and discovery, making the arts a truly integral part of a child's education.[89]

Schubart told the Lincoln Center board: "It is not sufficient to expose children to the performing arts." What was needed, he said, was an institute that would train teachers, work with artists interested in educating children, create presentations geared specifically to children, and disseminate its expertise. "Lincoln Center is able to provide the artistic resources," he argued. "Now it is necessary to find people and groups who wish to work with the Center."[90]

Schubart's vision gained the support of Father Laurence J. McGinley, the then president of Fordham University and an original Lincoln Center director. Despite some concern among constituent members that the proposed effort could threaten their own outreach efforts, the board of directors agreed in 1974 to a three-year development phase of what would be known formally as the Lincoln Center Institute for the Arts in Education, provided that "funding for this phase can be found, in advance, from non-competitive sources."[91] In arguing the case for the Institute, Francis Keppel, a well-known educator and subsequently the Institute's first chairman, said, "For fourteen years, the Lincoln Center Student Program has been working to bring a better understanding of the arts to young people and to integrate this concept into the school curriculum." It is now clear, he added, that "the key to this effort lies in the training of teachers."[92]

In the process of conceptualizing the program, Schubart had consulted Maxine Greene—a professor of philosophy and education at Teacher's College, Columbia University—who would become an integral part of the Institute. Schubart had first imagined that the

Institute would teach such things as what makes a work of art (sound, light, time, motion) and what an artist does. Students would also participate in improvisation and attend performances in studios.[93]

June Dunbar, a former dancer and teacher at Juilliard who became Schubart's artistic director and second in command at the Institute, remembered, "We were struggling with how to put into language what it was that teachers would learn. We'd worked out something we called a grid, an educational grid, in which there were certain components of the arts that we felt would have to be understood by teachers. Maxine Greene swept in like a high wind and said, 'Stop! That will never work, because you're imposing things on people that are rigid and prescriptive, and if there's anything that is germane to the arts at all, if there's anything that the arts embody wholeheartedly, it's a new experience every time you encounter a work of art. Therefore, use the work of art itself as the focus for study.'"[94]

Greene's understanding of aesthetic education became the driving force behind the new Institute's program. Its primary focus was the development of children. "What we want to teach them is how to see and how to hear, so that they'll never look at things in quite the same way again," said Schubart.[95] In articulating this view, he challenged what had been the orthodoxy in arts education. "Being exposed, and only exposed, doesn't mean you're learning anything; it means that you're a captive audience," Dunbar explained.[96] Instead, children would learn through active engagement with the work of art itself, from which concepts could then be extrapolated.

The Institute had to enlist, and in some way educate, classroom teachers who would carry out the program—another revolutionary notion. Dunbar recalled, "One of the feelings we had early on was that unless teachers felt deeply about their own experiences in the arts, they could not discuss with authenticity ideas with students. Unless they were involved, they couldn't draw students out similarly. . . . What really appealed to me about [the whole idea] was

Lincoln Center Institute's Mark Schubart (with striped tie), flanked by June Dunbar on his immediate left and Maxine Greene on his immediate right, and surrounded by the Institute's 1978 teaching artists and participating teachers.

that teachers would become partners in the process. My gut feeling was that those teachers who really got involved would be changed as teachers."[97] They would learn to appreciate children's imaginative responses and not be looking for right or wrong answers.

Schubart and his colleagues at the Institute fashioned a plan of action and secured partial funding for the three-year pilot from the National Endowment for the Humanities. They experimented as they felt their way. In 1975, for instance, they tried running teacher workshops in participating schools at the end of the school day but found that the teachers were exhausted and the end results consequently were disappointing. So they proposed instead a summer session during which teachers—and not only art teachers but also math teachers, social studies teachers, English teachers—would come to Lincoln Center to study and explore works of art performed live especially for them. In this way, it was hoped, they would gain a personal appreciation not only for aesthetic education in general but also for the unique qualities in specific works. They would then take this appreciation back to their own classrooms and share all the excitement and joy that aesthetic education generates.

In July 1976, forty-seven teachers from eleven schools and four Institute-trained teaching artists signed on for the first three-week summer session at Lincoln Center. Among the works presented for study were Act II of Verdi's *La Traviata*, Stravinsky's *Marva*, a production of *The Threepenny Opera* starring Blair Brown, and *The Leaves Are Fading*, performed by the American Ballet Theatre, all with commentary provided by designers and theater artists. "The first summer session was heady, to say the least," recalled June Dunbar. "It was euphoric. People were very excited about being in the presence of real artists, real people who are working on aesthetic problems daily, where processes were different from their own, people who weren't thinking in pedagogical terms."[98]

Mark Schubart never looked back. "It was an absolutely astonishing experience. . . . We began hearing at that time what we now hear all the time, which is teachers saying things like, 'You've changed my life. You've changed the way I teach.'"[99] The Institute eventually developed units of study, each featuring a specific work of art and involving six or more classroom sessions. Different works were offered every year to constantly challenge participating teachers to think and dig and find exciting new ideas to bring into their classrooms.

Teachers selected a unit they wished to study during the summer at Lincoln Center. Then, together with Institute-trained teaching artists, they taught that particular work to their students during the following school year. "The point was that the teachers wouldn't be sent back to the schools to fend alone," said June Dunbar. "Instead of being thrown into the ocean and told to swim, we would support them by having teaching artists go out and work with their classrooms."[100]

Over the years, Dunbar, Schubart, and their staff at the Institute worked hard at recruiting and retaining a dedicated and talented corps of teaching artists—actors, dancers, musicians, and visual artists—and a varied, challenging, and occasionally controversial repertory of works. Giving students a first-rate experience in the arts was the top priority. "To really shock them and open them up to beauty, to power, to understanding, to human responses—that has been my credo as artistic director," said Dunbar, "and Mark allowed me to do that because he trusted me."[101] Works as different as *Krapp's Last Tape*, by Samuel Beckett, or Institute commissions like Peter Parnell's *Scooter Thomas Makes It to the Top of the World* or Jean Anouilh's *Antigone*, set in a Third World country, brought electricity to the process of discovering ideas within these works that children might not otherwise encounter.

In 1991, the Institute moved into its own quarters in the new Rose Building, a facility that afforded first-rate rehearsal and performance spaces, as well as an impressive resource center to house the Institute's large collection of reference and circulating materials. The move also coincided with an expansion of the Institute's programs, occasioned by a $3.2 million grant from the Lila Wallace–Reader's Digest Fund to evaluate—along with Harvard's

Dance Around the World, a performance piece from the Lincoln Center Institute Summer Session, 1986.

Project Zero and Teachers College, Columbia University—the impact of the Institute and its work. The five-year research and development project determined that the Institute should expand upon three areas that made it a leader in its field: teacher education, program intensity, and artistic quality.[102] In response, the Institute put in place new programs, including the Focus Schools Collaborative, which involves all students and teachers in a particular school; the Higher Education Collaborative, to include college teachers; and a wider mix of year-round professional development opportunities.

And what about the revolution in arts education?

Beginning with forty-seven teachers that first summer, the Institute had welcomed, by the year 2001, its twenty-fifth anniversary, some two thousand educators—registrants, auditors, and visitors. In the process, it had turned away many applicants it was unable to accommodate. Its cadre of teaching artists included more than a hundred active participants, and its repertory—in dance, music, theater, the visual arts, and architecture—was considered to be among the most exciting ever. Equally impressive was the fact that the Institute had fashioned something of an international movement, having been replicated by twenty other organizations across the country and overseas, all now under the umbrella of the Association of Institutes for Aesthetic Education.

Mark Schubart stepped down as executive director of the Lincoln Center Institute in 1995 and was succeeded by Scott Noppe-Brandon. When Schubart died in 2000, he was eulogized at Lincoln Center as a true visionary who "transformed the way that students and teachers interact with the arts by building the Lincoln Center Institute for the Arts in Education into one of the nation's leading arts in education organizations. Under his nurturing leadership, the Institute's success grew into an international movement with a network of affiliated institutions across the country and overseas."[103]

Noppe-Brandon brought both experience and enthusiasm to his position as executive director. "We've been able to show that the arts and the aesthetic dimension, in and through the pedagogy we support, can have an impact in all teaching and learning in a school, so that the arts are not marginalized," Noppe-Brandon remarked. "We've been a catalyst for that conversation, to connect the arts to the broader needs of teaching and learning in the whole school."[104] As for the future, his goals included continuing to develop the Focus Schools Collaborative and Teacher in Education efforts while growing the number of Association of Institutes for Aesthetic Education members worldwide. He also pointed to the Lincoln Center Institute's ongoing exploration of the appropriate role of technology in the expansion of its program.[105] In May 2006, the Institute announced the launch of its Imagination Award, a competition designed to honor one New York City school each year that excels at utilizing and inspiring imagination in its classrooms.[106]

Typically threatened in times of budgetary crises with their inevitable political questions about relevancy, arts education in all its forms has struggled to survive, most noticeably in the public schools, where it is often the first program to be cut. Yet the basic premise behind the work of the Institute—that aesthetic awareness challenges all children to learn about, and through, the arts—decrees the arts as indispensable to the learning process. The performance artist John Kelly noted that the Lincoln Center Institute has "provided a fresh and immensely workable alternative to traditional arts education and, where it has succeeded in penetrating the entrenched educational bureaucracies, has changed the way arts are taught, learned and experienced in schools today."[107]

3

THE CHANGING CAMPUS

Architecture and Art Serve the Community

THE LINCOLN CENTER CAMPUS, AS IT WAS ORIGINALLY conceived, was completed in 1969. Only in the early 1980s did Lincoln Center embark, under chairman Martin E. Segal's leadership, on an additional building project—the Samuel B. and David Rose Building, which was completed in 1990, during George Weissman's chairmanship. It provided more space, such as dormitories for students of the Juilliard School and the School of American Ballet, and needed amenities for many of its resident organizations. The

The Lincoln Center campus festively aglow during the winter holidays.

campus and its halls have also undergone changes, some noticeable, some not. The inclusion of the visual arts on campus has enriched and enlivened the aesthetic experience of all who visit Lincoln Center.

The Rose Building

Well before the 1969 completion of the last of the original Lincoln Center buildings, the Center's founders recognized that future expansion was inevitable, if only to realize elements of the original plan—such as dormitories for the Juilliard School—that had been too expensive to include initially.[1]

In February 1966, anticipating the need for future growth, Lincoln Center executed a previously negotiated "Agreement with the City of New York," under which Lincoln Center would have the option to eventually purchase the High School of Commerce site (later to become known as the Brandeis High School Annex), on the northeast corner of Amsterdam Avenue and 65th Street, and an additional parcel on the southeast corner of 66th Street and Amsterdam. Lincoln Center would be called upon to exercise this option at such time as the Board of Education decided to vacate the school.

The "Agreement" included a formula for computing the price Lincoln Center would have to pay. John D. Rockefeller 3rd set aside funds that could be used toward this future purchase.[2] Lincoln

Brandeis High School Annex, site of the future Samuel B. and David Rose Building, October 1986.

Center hoped to one day erect a school building, an office, and a dormitory tower building on the site.[3]

Pressure to expand intensified in the mid-1970s, driven by the Center's growing audiences and increasingly popular offerings. Every nook and cranny of available space was being used, often for purposes not originally intended. Juilliard, for example, wanted to reclaim the studio rehearsal space it had leased to the School of American Ballet in 1969. Juilliard also yearned for a more campus-like setting, with safe, comfortable dormitories, so that the most talented students would continue to be drawn there. But Juilliard was not alone. Many resident organizations needed additional office, storage, and rehearsal space. The Film Society and the Lincoln Center Institute dreamed of having auditoriums designed especially for their programs.

Since expansion seemed inevitable, it was best to be prepared. Chairman Amyas Ames, Martin E. Segal, and the Center's other leaders turned for advice first to Richard H. Koch, a lawyer who had helped to devise the Museum of Modern Art's innovative sale of air rights to fund its Museum Tower expansion a few years earlier. Koch conducted a needs assessment for the Center and its constituents, then submitted a plan of action. He identified a large parcel of land immediately to the west of Juilliard as the best place to construct a combined-use building, which would include dormitories, rehearsal studios, offices, storage space, and a garage for patrons. The key to Koch's plan was a residential apartment tower that could attract a significant capital investment and provide a permanent revenue stream.[4]

The Lincoln Center board reviewed Koch's feasibility study at its December 1980 meeting and voted to proceed, in principle, with the project. Amyas Ames then appointed a New Building Committee, led by Richard Shinn, the chairman and CEO of Metropolitan Life, to oversee all related activities and expenditures. When Martin E. Segal succeeded Ames as chairman in June 1981, he asked the committee to begin to consider the issues—land acquisition, demolition, construction, and financing—that would have to be resolved quickly once the property became available.

Segal's foresight soon paid off. In September 1982, the Board of Education informed Lincoln Center that it would vacate the Brandeis High School Annex in the fall of 1983. Once Lincoln Center took ownership, it would have only six months to demolish the structure. That was a fairly easy requirement to address, but in order to avoid living for years with a rubble-strewn lot, Segal hoped to see a new building rise as quickly as possible. He suggested that the committee retain the architect David Kenneth Specter as a consultant to outline what needed to be done and to expedite matters. Specter and members of the committee immediately began to explore "the space needs of the constituents and Lincoln Center and how these needs could be accommodated in view of the architectural, structural, aesthetic and financial requirements for the building and the governmental approval process."[5] In view of this initial role he was asked to play, Specter graciously agreed that he would not be a candidate for architect of whatever project would eventually be built.

The committee presented its recommendations to the Lincoln Center board at the December 1983 board meeting. Frederick P. Rose—the prominent New York real-estate developer, philanthropist, and New York Philharmonic board member, whom Segal had recruited to serve on the New Building Committee at its inception—assumed chairmanship of the committee when Richard Shinn resigned to work on other aspects of the project. Rose's presentation described the individual elements of the project: a base building of approximately 200,000 square feet with many shared facilities; an apartment tower to be built by a developer to whom Lincoln Center would sell its air rights from the Brandeis High School Annex site and adjacent Lincoln Center property; and a possible garage facility. At the conclusion of Rose's presentation, the board authorized the New Building Committee to proceed with all steps necessary to acquire the annex site and construct a new building.

Among other actions taken that day, the board appointed an architectural selection subcommittee consisting of Segal, Rose, Gordon J. Davis, and Howard Stein, the chairman and CEO of the Dreyfus Corporation; approved hiring an environmental review consultant; and authorized the retention of Lord, Day & Lord, Davis's law firm, to provide legal services in connection with the new building.[6]

The December 1983 board meeting marked the beginning of a frenetic period during which the purchase agreement with the city had to be negotiated and the complicated city approvals process navigated. At the same time, the Center's leadership had to refine Richard Koch's needs assessment, legally commit all participants to the building project, select the architect, and develop a fund-raising plan. This was a daunting agenda, but much of it was accomplished in less than a year.

By the late fall of 1984, the participating resident organizations had reached tentative agreements on space usage and the allocation of costs for the schematic design phase. The board also ratified the selection of the architectural team of Davis Brody & Associates and Abramowitz, Harris, Kingsland. According to Segal, the two firms "made a deep impression on the interviewing committee in presenting the beautiful and farsighted idea of opening the Juilliard School out into Lincoln Center,"[7] an innovative plan that would successfully integrate the new building with the rest of the campus.

Negotiations with the city for the land dragged on for longer than expected. Based on the original "Agreement," Lincoln Center expected to pay the city approximately $3.5 million for the Brandeis High School Annex site and the adjacent lot. Instead, the city—still reeling from its fiscal crisis of the 1970s—suggested $15 million. Segal recalled that "Mayor Koch and I had some words, during which I pointed to the 'Agreement' and the formula that Lincoln Center had reached with the city in 1966. The mayor refused to budge. I went to see Deputy Mayor Kenneth Lipper, who really understood the issues and helped us sway the mayor."[8]

Eventually, they settled on a price of $6 million for the sites and certain development rights to an adjacent firehouse (which Lincoln Center, Inc., later agreed to relocate during construction and subsequently rehouse in its new building). Mayor Koch signed the contract on behalf of the city on the occasion of Lincoln Center's twenty-fifth anniversary celebration, October 22, 1984.

A great deal remained to be done. The year 1985 was one of constant negotiations—between Lincoln Center management and the constituents, as well as between Lincoln Center and various organs of city government and the architectural team. Segal and Rose, who by this time had been elected a director of Lincoln Center and who would later serve as board vice chairman, effectively moved these discussions along toward resolution. "I cannot overemphasize the importance of the leadership of Martin Segal at this point, and the practical knowledge, experience, and wisdom of Fred Rose," said Gordon J. Davis. "By the time the building project really began to move in 1983–84, there wasn't an institution at Lincoln Center that wasn't bursting at the seams with some unmet need for space of some kind." Davis recalled that Segal "proposed that the building be undertaken on the basis that each institution would get according to and give according to need, and pay expenses according to the amount of space in the new building—the percentage of total space—it would occupy."[9]

One of the knottiest issues Lincoln Center faced was reaching a satisfactory agreement with the participating resident organizations on how to allocate annual operating costs for the new building and on deciding who would own it. Until those basic matters were settled, little else could be done. Ongoing negotiations finally resulted in an agreement that the Lincoln Center board ratified on October 7, 1985.

Under the terms of the agreement, these resident organizations agreed to share maintenance costs on a proportionate basis throughout the life of the building and to allocate the proceeds from the sale of the air rights on the same basis. Each of the participants also accepted responsibility for the management and the maintenance of its own space. Finally, all participants agreed that Lincoln Center, Inc., would manage the project and own the completed building after providing each of them with a ninety-nine-year lease.[10]

Another decision made at that board meeting proved to be critical to the project's ultimate success: Segal, with the support of Fred Rose, urged Lincoln Center to forgo an equity position in the condominium apartment building, thus limiting its exposure to the vagaries of the real-estate market. (As subsequent events were to prove, the decision to forgo an equity interest and to sell the air rights turned out most fortuitously, because the residential tower project as originally conceived went bankrupt in 1992. A new developer, L. C. Associates, undertook the successful completion of the building.[11])

With these issues resolved, events began to move swiftly. The Center board approved the New Building Committee's unanimous recommendation to hire the Stillman Group as the developer of both the Center's building and the residential tower. After lively discussion about its potential financial risks, the board approved the inclusion of a five-level garage to provide for the longer-term parking needs of Lincoln Center patrons.

The Capital Campaign

During the course of 1985, the architects finalized their design and refined the formal Request for Proposals to send to potential developers. Lincoln Center's leadership also began to think about how the project would be financed and formulated plans for a coordinated approach to fund-raising to which all participating constituents agreed.

George Weissman, who succeeded Segal as chairman of Lincoln Center in 1986, worked with the board members Willard C. Butcher (the then chairman and CEO of the Chase Manhattan Bank), Richard

Shinn, and Frederick P. Rose on the $100 million fund-raising campaign to finance the building and provide an endowment for operations. The sale of the development rights to the Stillman Group yielded $48,525,000, with the remainder of the cost of the new building to be raised from corporations, foundations, and individual donors, as well as an anticipated donation from the City of New York. Even with nearly 50 percent of the total in hand, this constituted an arduous undertaking. "We decided we didn't have the staff or the experience for a major capital campaign fund drive," remembered George Weissman. "We hired the firm of Brakeley, John Price Jones, Inc., which had done a lot of fund-raising for non-profit institutions,"[12] to organize the effort. Butcher, Shinn, and Rose, however, together with Segal and Weissman, all assumed the principal burden for fund-raising.

Lincoln Center broke ground for its new building on November 10, 1987. "Wearing a hard hat that warded off nothing more perilous than a cold, windy rain, the chairman of Lincoln Center, George Weissman, held the same shovel that President Eisenhower used to break ground for Lincoln Center in 1959,"[13] reported the *New York Times*. Speaking for the entire Lincoln Center community, Weissman announced, "Our buildings are beautiful and graceful, but our great achievement is the environment these buildings create for the performing arts—the sounds and movements that emanate, the dreams they nurture and fulfill."[14]

Ground breaking marked the beginning of the public phase of the fund-raising campaign. In addition to the proceeds from the sale of development rights, Lincoln Center obtained pledges of more than $30 million, including $10.1 million from the City of New York, a $15 million anonymous gift, and $2 million each from the Rita J. and Stanley H. Kaplan Foundation, the Fan Fox and Leslie R. Samuels Foundation, and the DeWitt Wallace Fund.

Frederick P. Rose and his wife, Sandra, were identified at a June 1990 press conference as the donors of the anonymous $15 million gift. Rose remembered, "We realized, and the fund-raisers said so,

Ground-breaking ceremony for the Rose Building, November 10, 1987. Lincoln Center chairman George Weissman holds the ceremonial shovel.

that we'd have one lead gift of $15 million. My wife and I have a foundation which supports our philanthropic efforts, and I said this would be the perfect memorial for my Uncle Dave and for Dad, who worked together as a team. Sandy and I thought it would be an appropriate memorial." Fred Rose and his wife set one condition: "It must be anonymous until the job is finished. . . . It was much easier to make the strongest possible appeal for an anonymous building"[15] in his capacity as a cochairman of the New Building Campaign.

The campaign ran into difficulties. The recession of the late 1980s negatively impacted charitable giving, and Lincoln Center had to compete with many other organizations for limited philanthropic dollars. Completion of the $100 million drive proved a challenge. (A total of $25 million was initially intended for the building's endowment, but ultimately all the money raised went toward completion of the building, which had encountered significant cost overruns.) However, with the receipt in December 1991 of a very generous $5 million gift from the family of the late *Music Man* composer Meredith Willson to name the Juilliard residence tower in his memory, the campaign all but met its $100 million goal.

Dealing with the City

At the same time that Lincoln Center was dealing with the architectural, financial, and internal administrative questions related to the Rose Building, it was struggling with the cumbersome regulations and approvals processes the city had enacted to control all real-estate developments. Few of these procedures had been in place during the 1950s and the first half of the 1960s—the heyday of "urban renewal"—when Lincoln Center had been conceived and constructed. In fact, it was the real or imagined abuses associated with the initial phase of "slum clearance" in New York City, controlled by the redoubtable Robert Moses, that had led to the imposition of many of the safeguards (or obstacles) regulating development, which Lincoln Center now had to resolve before proceeding with its project.

All developers had to adhere to the city's Uniform Land Use Review Procedure (ULURP). Once the City Planning Commission certified the documents Lincoln Center submitted to it in March 1986, there were a mere six months during which the entire ULURP process had to be completed. Lincoln Center president Nathan Leventhal and board member Gordon J. Davis, both of whom had had extensive experience in city government, helped the project through what Leventhal later described as "the usual brutal process"[16] of Community Board, City Planning Commission, and

Board of Estimate hearings. The building plans met with initial community opposition, but two short-lived lawsuits were both successfully disposed of. The City Planning Commission approved the addition but asked Lincoln Center to reduce the size of the tower by seventy-five feet, which it did. ULURP's final stop was the Board of Estimate hearing on August 14, 1986, which turned into a thirteen-hour marathon of testimony by both proponents and opponents of the project, after which the board gave Lincoln Center the official go-ahead.

Workers "topped out" the building in July 1989 and worked to finish the dormitory section in time for occupancy in the fall of 1990. Construction delays and cost overruns plagued completion of the five-level garage, however. Furthermore, Lincoln Center had difficulty finding a suitable operator for the parking facility but finally extended a long-term lease to the Mallah Organization for this purpose.

Completion

On November 19, 1990, amid much fanfare and mutual congratulations among all those who had made the project possible, the Samuel B. and David Rose Building at Lincoln Center was officially dedicated at a ceremony in the New York State Theater. (The Rose Building would not be fully occupied until the spring of 1991.) Most of the Center's administrative activities were now located under one roof, in the new, multiple-function building. The Rose Building provided residence halls for students of Juilliard and the School of American Ballet, as well as performance, rehearsal, and office space for its tenants. Included in the ten-story, 235,000-square-foot institutional portion of the building were

- the 268-seat Walter Reade Theater for the Film Society of Lincoln Center;
- a student/artist center and a dining hall for students of the Juilliard School and the School for American Ballet;

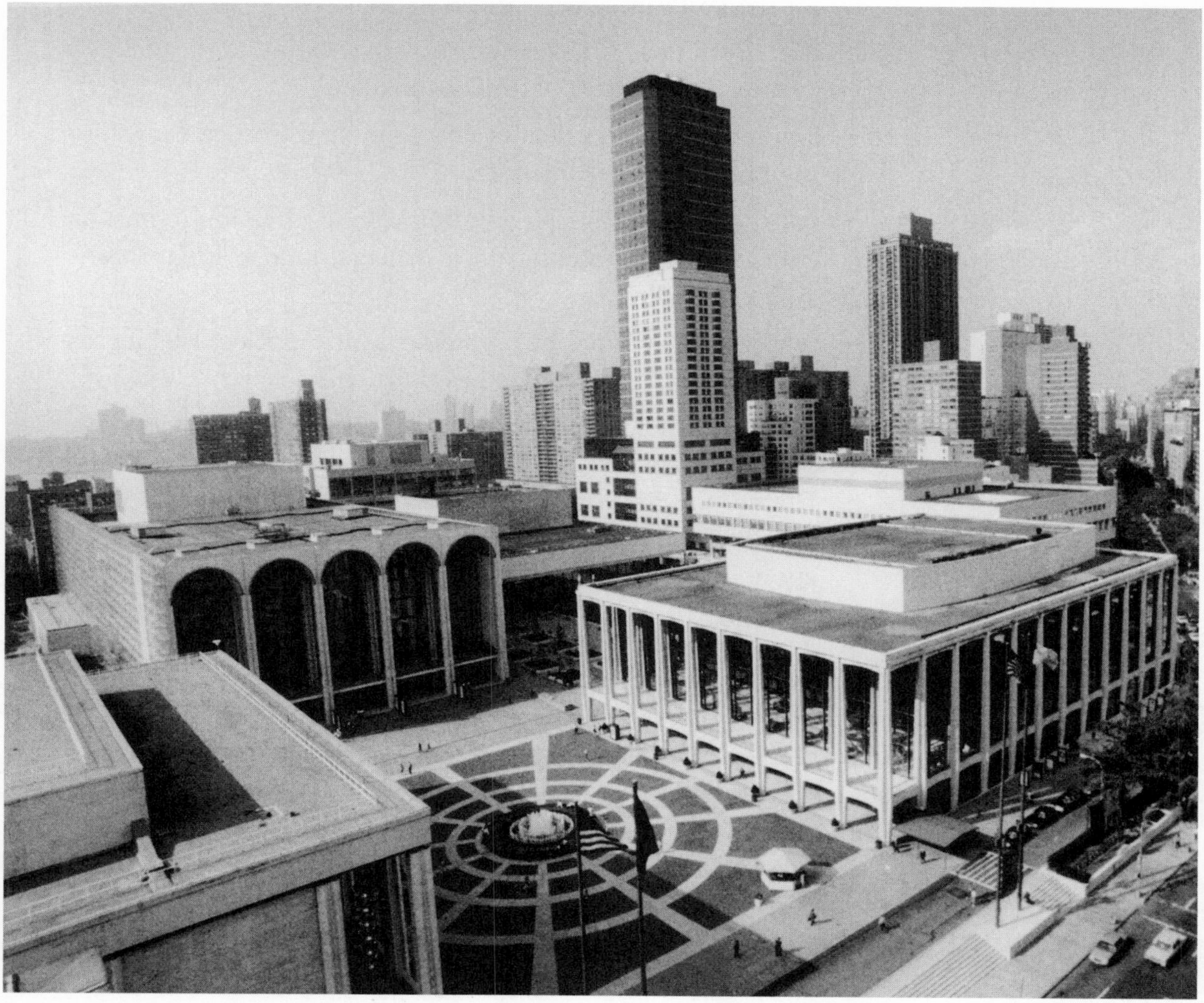

The expanded Lincoln Center campus, upon completion
of the Samuel B. and David Rose Building; photo c. 1993.

- production facilities for *Live from Lincoln Center*;
- archives for the New York Philharmonic and Lincoln Center for the Performing Arts, Inc.;
- dance studios, classrooms, dressing rooms, and ancillary space for the School of American Ballet;
- a workshop/studio theater and a library/resource center for the Lincoln Center Institute;
- ballet rehearsal studios, a costume shop, dressing rooms, an education department, and a dancers' lounge for the New York City Ballet;
- rehearsal space for the Chamber Music Society of Lincoln Center;
- office and management facilities for the Film Society, the School of American Ballet, the City Center of Music and Drama, the Metropolitan Opera Guild, the Lincoln Center Institute, the New York City Ballet, the Chamber Music Society, and Lincoln Center for the Performing Arts, Inc.;
- the Riverside Branch of the New York Public Library;
- a new home for the New York City Fire Department's Engine Company 40 and Ladder Company 35.

Above the ten-story base stood an eighteen-story, 115,000-square-foot residence hall tower for students of the Juilliard School and the School of American Ballet.[17]

The Rose Building was warmly received by many observers, who felt it successfully addressed many of Lincoln Center's needs and concerns. The architecture critic and writer Paul Goldberger called it "a stunning addition" to the Lincoln Center campus. The architects had created a functional multiuse space that satisfied the needs of what were, in effect, eleven separate clients. They were also able to create the illusion of two separate buildings by setting the condominium tower back and covering it with a different material than was used on the Lincoln Center portion of the building. "It doesn't quite disappear," commented Goldberger, referring to the condominium tower, "but it is about as deferential as a sixty-story skyscraper can be. . . . . From a distance, it all works, and the two buildings appear to be distinct and only distantly related."[18]

To the principal architect Lewis Davis, however, the key to the project had been moving Juilliard's entrance from 66th Street to the newly created promenade above 65th Street, thereby linking the building and the North Plaza surrounding it to the rest of the Lincoln Center campus. Building upon an existing but essentially unused bridge over 65th Street, he located on that promenade not only the new Juilliard entrance but also the school's bookstore, ticket office, and admissions office, as well as the new Walter Reade Theater. These additions infused the promenade with activity. Before, explained Davis, "Juilliard students could go there for four years and never know there was a Lincoln Center." His plan allowed the North Plaza and the promenade to "become flooded with kids, to become their campus. Every time they walk into or leave Juilliard, they are exposed to the places they really want to wind up in—Avery Fisher Hall, the Beaumont, the Met, New York State Theater."[19]

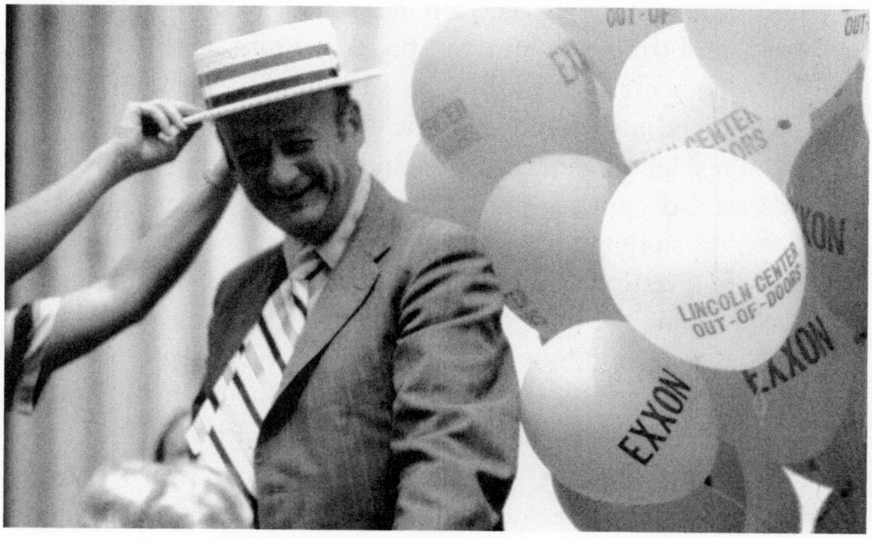

New York City mayor Edward I. Koch, whose enthusiastic support of Lincoln Center helped bring to fruition the Samuel B. and David Rose building project, at Lincoln Center, August 1978.

Furthermore, the plan was community-friendly. "A wonderful thing that Marty Segal and Nat Leventhal picked up on was the policy that Lincoln Center should really be open to the neighborhood. . . . They both felt that the students from Martin Luther King, Jr. High School and LaGuardia High School of the Performing Arts [located on Amsterdam Avenue, directly opposite the Center] and other community people should have full access to the promenade. So we provided stairs to make the Bridge Plaza accessible from Amsterdam Avenue."[20]

What secured the ultimate success of the building project? One important element was the favorable financial arrangement Lincoln Center was able to negotiate for itself. Lincoln Center chose to take the $48,525,000 outright from the Stillman Group for the sale of its development rights and to eschew future financial participation in the commercial enterprise. Second, in anticipation of so doing, Lincoln Center decided to sell the developer the building "as of right," which meant it would take the project through the city's approvals process before the sale, which made it much more attractive to the developer.[21] A third important element was the strong and consistent support of Mayor Edward I. Koch during the planning and construction phases of the project. Upon Koch's leaving office in 1989, the board paid tribute to him and presented him with a section of the limestone being used in the construction of the new building.

The last, and maybe most significant, element was the ability of the eleven resident organizations to find ways of coming together in the successful occupancy and management of a complicated real-estate deal. In so doing, they demonstrated the kind of cooperation and cross-fertilization the founders had dreamed of when the idea of Lincoln Center was put on paper for the first time in the mid-1950s. The new building project "had the very beneficial effect that—for the first time, really, since the construction of Lincoln Center—all the constituents worked together with Lincoln Center to build the new building," noted George Weissman.[22] (The Lincoln Center Theater and the Metropolitan Opera did not participate, although the Metropolitan Opera Guild did.) "The ability to do the Mozart Bicentennial [1991–1992], in which all the constituents participated, is an example of how the cooperation spawned by the new building project produced artistic benefits as well,"[23] added Gordon J. Davis.

Martin E. Segal best summarized the process: "When I signed the contract with the city to acquire the land, everybody said, 'We'll never get this done.' Look what happened in the course of four years. Dormitories for the Juilliard students, dormitories for the students of the School of American Ballet, new offices, rehearsal space, new facilities for Juilliard. . . . Nearly $100 million was raised to accomplish that."[24]

The Rose Building, the first addition to the original Lincoln Center campus, had been a cooperative venture of daunting proportions, and it had succeeded beyond what many would have dared to dream.

The New York State Theater

The acoustics in the New York State Theater always worked well for one of its resident companies: the New York City Ballet. Reputedly, nary a footfall could be heard. But opinions differed on how well the spoken word and vocal music were projected to some parts of the hall. These concerns led to the installation of an amplification system for the hall's opening night—April 23, 1964—but with mixed results.[25] The following month, Peter Brook directed the Royal Shakespeare Company's production of *King Lear* in the New York State Theater and publicly questioned the acoustics.[26]

In some ways, the criticisms by Brook and others should not have been surprising. Philip Johnson, with the active participation of New York City Ballet's two founders, George Balanchine and Lincoln Kirstein, had designed the theater most specifically for ballet. Balanchine and Kirstein, according to Johnson, "always

Opening night of the New York State Theater, April 23, 1964. Left to right: Richard Rodgers, head of Music Theater at Lincoln Center, with CBS newsman Robert Trout; New York State Theater architect Philip Johnson; and New York City Ballet's Lincoln Kirstein, George Balanchine, and Jacques d'Amboise.

thought it was the best theater in the world. . . . For them, it worked: onstage, backstage, and acoustics never came up."[27]

For the hall's other resident companies—Music Theater at Lincoln Center (until its effective demise in 1970) and the New York City Opera—however, the hall's acoustics were to prove less than ideal, although preliminary tests in September 1964 for future operatic performances were deemed more than acceptable by Lincoln Center personnel. Schuyler Chapin, Lincoln Center's vice president in charge of programming, told the *New York Times*: "Basically, it is a marvelous opera house. It needs no artificial amplification."[28] Nonetheless, in the ensuing years, a number of small modifications were introduced, and these did improve the acoustics for the New York City Opera, which had presented its first production there in early 1966 to mixed acoustical reviews.

These incremental changes satisfied few people, and when Beverly Sills assumed the City Opera's leadership in 1981, she made an acoustical overhaul one of her first priorities.[29] City Opera retained Dr. Cyril Harris, one of the world's outstanding acousticians, to study the theater and make recommendations. Working with Philip Johnson and his partner, John Burgee, Harris identified several problems, including the proscenium arch—all of which, in his opinion, could be remedied.[30]

In May 1981, the Fan Fox and Leslie R. Samuels Foundation announced that it would fund a $4 million renovation of the house, which Harris and Johnson would supervise.[31] Lincoln Center management was excited by the prospect. "The reconstruction of the State Theater . . . will add to the prestige of Lincoln Center by attracting the leading artists, be helpful to other constituents and further activities such as *Live from Lincoln Center*," they said.[32] New York City provided supplemental funds, which paid for additional seats, new flooring under the seats, and new aisle carpeting.[33] The renovation included a new concrete-and-steel ceiling, a reshaped proscenium, and wooden reflectors installed on the side and rear walls. The project came in on time and within budget, and most observers were pleased with the results. "I thought the acoustics had certainly improved," recalled Philip Johnson. "There's no doubt that they're better than they were. . . . The pit is larger, and the stage arch has been reversed."[34] Still, some people criticized the result, and, shortly after Paul Kellogg took over in 1996 as general manager and artistic director, City Opera announced that it was contemplating yet another acoustical makeover, albeit a modest one.

As joint tenants of the New York State Theater, both the City Opera and the New York City Ballet had to agree to any changes. "In some ways our acoustical concerns conflict," stated Sherwin Goldman, the executive producer in charge of the Opera's administration and finances. "We want to improve the projection of sound from the stage, but they [the Ballet] don't want their audiences to hear footfalls. Also, Philip Johnson, the architect, is known to have strong opinions about things. We had to think about how to approach the Fan Fox and Leslie R. Samuels Foundation, which paid for the first renovation, and tell them that it didn't work out as well as we would have liked."[35]

Rather than the kinds of structural solutions previously undertaken, the new changes amounted to only "a sound-enhancement system" featuring a series of microphones and speakers installed in strategic places throughout the hall. By the time they were unveiled in fall of 1999, "an informal survey of operagoers over the last few weeks seemed to indicate that many regulars didn't notice a difference, or thought the sound had improved,"[36] reported the *New York Times*. While some critics questioned the benefits of the latest acoustical fix, audiences and subscribers continued to enjoy the New York City Opera, perhaps reflecting what former Lincoln Center president William Schuman purportedly quipped: that acoustics are "nothing but hearsay."

Lincoln Center's decision at the end of 1999 to embark on a redevelopment program encouraged the City Opera to think about erecting a new building for itself somewhere on campus, a hall that would be designed specifically for its own needs. The City Ballet had seemed reluctant to permit the kind of structural alterations in the State Theater that the New York City Opera believed it required. For a while, Damrosch Park appeared to be a promising alternative site for a new opera house, but opposition to the idea by the Metropolitan Opera effectively killed it. It is also likely that there would have been significant community opposition to co-opting the park for a new hall.

Disappointed, the City Opera began to consider abandoning Lincoln Center for a new home somewhere else in the city. A $50 million pledge by the philanthropist Robert Wilson made the possibility seem more than an idle dream and effectively jump-started the organization's efforts to identify an appropriate site.

The City Opera's possible defection from the Lincoln Center campus raised troubling potential financial issues for the New York City Ballet, the theater's other permanent tenant. The two organizations shared the hall's operating expenses, and the loss of one would prove difficult not only for the remaining tenant but also for Lincoln Center itself, which, as landlord, would have to find a suitable replacement.

During 2001, the City Opera looked at possible locations for a new house, including Donald Trump's Riverside project on the far West Side. Then, in the aftermath of the collapse of the World Trade Center towers on September 11, 2001, it appeared there might be an opportunity to relocate the Opera in the newly rebuilt downtown. The Lower Manhattan Development Corporation wanted to include a "performing-arts complex," the tenants to be determined, and the New York City Opera began to pursue seriously the possibility of relocating there. "The most important thing for City Opera at this stage in its history is to have its own home," said Paul Kellogg. "We're at the stage where we can blossom, but we need a house with good acoustics and the right size, and a schedule we can determine ourselves."[37]

While Lincoln Center management urged the New York City Opera to remain on campus, Paul Kellogg and his board were increasingly drawn to the idea of relocating downtown. For two years, they worked to secure a place there, engaging architects and financial advisers to assist them in preparing their proposal. For a time, it appeared they had "the inside track on becoming the cultural anchor at the World Trade Center site."[38] But then, in a move that reportedly took the Opera by surprise, the Lower Manhattan Development Corporation opened things up by "inviting arts groups from all over the world to submit proposals, suggesting that a place for City Opera is not secured."[39]

Robert Wilson, the Opera's major benefactor, did not support a move downtown, fearing that its audience would not follow, and withdrew his $50 million offer.[40] It then appeared that the New York City Opera would have difficulty securing the funding necessary to build and thereafter sustain a new house downtown. In addition, there was significant community opposition to the idea of including opera, considered an "elitist" medium, in the downtown mix.

These uncertainties proved to be too much for the Lower Manhattan Development Corporation. In June 2004, it rejected the New York City Opera's proposal to move to ground zero. Mayor Michael Bloomberg, a former Lincoln Center director, also opposed the deal, arguing that the City Opera was "an economic linchpin of the city-owned New York State Theater." He reportedly asked, "If you take away my tenant, who is going to pay the rent?"[41]

The New York City Opera continued to look at possible venues for a new house. One site—the current home of the New York City chapter of the American Red Cross on Amsterdam Avenue at 66th Street—appeared especially promising. It would have ensured the continued presence of the New York City Opera at Lincoln Center, extending the geographic boundaries of the campus northward and westward. Robert Wilson, in a nod to the appeal of the Red Cross site, renewed his $50 million pledge.[42] Negotiations with the site's developer, A. & R. Kalimian Realty, brought the Opera almost to the point of an official agreement, so much so that on April 27, 2006, the City Opera announced it was close to a deal. Certain "legal, financial and design issues" proved irresolvable, however, and less than a week later, the City Opera was once again weighing its relocation options, still hoping for a new home, one that would allow it to remain a part of the Lincoln Center family.

Avery Fisher Hall

When the completely renovated Avery Fisher Hall—for years troubled by criticisms of its acoustics—reopened on October 19, 1976, it was praised by musicians and critics alike. The composer and Philharmonic music director Pierre Boulez said the sound was now "very clean—precise—but not clinical. . . . The balance between woodwinds and strings is now very good."[43] Harold Schonberg, the *New York Times* music critic and a longtime skeptic about the acoustics of the old hall, wrote, "Had the jinx that afflicted the hall since it opened on September 23, 1962, been licked? The answer was quickly forthcoming. The national anthem was followed by Nathan Milstein and the Brahms Violin Concerto, and there was general happiness forty minutes later."[44] Schonberg thought the new hall had "much better bass sound, though traditionalists probably will want more color."[45] Donal Henahan of the *New York Times* compared performances by the New York Philharmonic of Mahler's

Third Symphony in both Carnegie Hall (where the Philharmonic was completing an earlier Mahler Festival) and in the new Avery Fisher Hall. He concluded that the "orchestra produced a splendid, satisfying sound in both halls."[46] Andrew Porter in the *New Yorker* added to the generally favorable critical response, writing that the sound was warm and that "the whole hall was resonant with sound." He concluded, "In short, unqualified initial approval for the acoustics of the new Fisher Hall."[47] Ada Louise Huxtable, also of the *Times*, added architectural praise for the hall's new interior.

As part of the 1976 renovation, the organ in the old hall was removed and eventually sold to the Crystal Cathedral in Los Angeles. Philharmonic president Carlos Moseley regretted the loss of the organ but testified that the acoustician, Dr. Cyril Harris, told him "there was absolutely no way, because of the structural supports of the building, that one could keep the organ space and not lose stage spaces."[48] Whether Harris believed that removing the organ would help the acoustics was not clear.

The Lincoln Center and New York Philharmonic managements basked in the apparent success of their efforts, and with the arrival of Zubin Mehta in 1979 as the Philharmonic's music director, there was general excitement as the orchestra began a new era in its renovated hall.

The first serious criticisms of the new Avery Fisher Hall came from some of the same people who had praised it earlier. In a *New York Times* article, Harold Schonberg noted, "Today, the hall is still not universally admired—it continues to lack bass—but it has amazing clarity and it is an infinite improvement over Philharmonic Hall."[49]

Some musicians also complained that they were unable to hear each other on stage, objecting to the strident brass and percussion sound coming off the reflective back wall. Zubin Mehta responded by rearranging the orchestra seating. He also convened the orchestra to discuss the matter. The string players wanted to move the orchestra out into the hall and have it surrounded by audience seats,

Avery Fisher Hall reopens after renovation on October 19, 1976.

while other musicians blamed the conductors for not controlling the brass sound. A few even suggested that the real culprit was the upholstery on the auditorium seats![50]

While there was clearly discontent, there was no clear pattern to the debate. In fact, Will Crutchfield, reporting on identical programs performed by the Vienna Philharmonic, concluded that "the Vienna Philharmonic sounded distinctly better in Fisher Hall than in Carnegie."[51]

The renewal of the controversy puzzled the Center's management. They maintained that the hall's acoustics, at least for the audience, were not a problem. Avery Fisher strongly supported this position. In late 1988, he wrote to George Weissman, the chairman of Lincoln Center, urging him to stand firm and noting, "We are dealing here with subjective opinions. It is an absolute minefield. In the case of the Philharmonic musicians, they were delighted with the hall when it reopened. They said so in writing four months after the reopening and after dozens of rehearsals and concerts—plenty of time to form a seasoned judgment." Fisher went on to say that "the hall has not changed, only their opinions. . . . Once we start tinkering with the hall, there will be no end to it."[52]

The acoustics issue went into abeyance with Zubin Mehta's announcement in late 1988 that he would end his music directorship when his contract expired in 1991. At the end of 1990, A. K. Webster also indicated that he would retire as executive director, so any discussion of acoustics would await new artistic and administrative leaders at the Philharmonic.

With Kurt Masur's appointment as music director in 1990, the debate renewed, especially in regard to onstage conditions. Masur explored the question of acoustical improvement and revisited the issue of reinstalling an organ similar to the one that had been removed during the 1976 renovation. He arranged to have another acoustical expert—Dr. Paul Badura-Skoda, with whom he had worked in Leipzig—examine the hall and make recommendations on both subjects.

Lincoln Center management became concerned about the public-relations impact of Masur's actions and sought to take control of the situation. In early February 1991, Avery Fisher met with Masur and other Philharmonic representatives. The new artistic director described his desire to deal with the musicians' complaints about hearing each other onstage, the need for an organ, and a flexible and reversible way of extending the stage for some performances.

The Center's management refused to rush "ahead with anything about acoustics" and so informed the Philharmonic's leadership. Lincoln Center president Nathan Leventhal told the acting executive director of the Philharmonic, Allison Vulgamore, that Lincoln Center's preference "would be that Masur live with the hall for a couple of years before he decides what needs to be done."[53] With Lincoln Center's agreement, the Philharmonic engaged the respected firm Jaffe Acoustics to do a binaural study and to survey the Philharmonic musicians. At the same time, the Philharmonic's representatives were eager to resolve the matter in a way that recognized Lincoln Center's concerns. At a meeting of the Lincoln Center board of directors, the Philharmonic's chairman, Stephen Stamas, insisted that "the Philharmonic's concern was to improve the musicians' hearing onstage and that the sound in the hall was fine."

Jaffe Acoustics proceeded with its work during the summer of 1991, but Lincoln Center board members and staff were skeptical. In a letter, Leventhal wondered whether the experiments with sound diffusion and the surveys would supply a useful result, especially since the Philharmonic's musicians had not fully participated in the surveys.[54] While Stamas sought to reassure Leventhal, counseling patience until the final results were known, he also laid down a strong marker by asserting that the Philharmonic believed the preliminary surveys had provided strong evidence of the need for change.[55]

As expected, the Jaffe report was inconclusive, but it did provide enough credible evidence to enable Masur to press ahead. Not, however, before yet another expert, Russell Johnson of Artec

Consultants, Inc., reviewed Jaffe's recommendations—a step suggested by the Philharmonic and accepted by Lincoln Center.

At a press conference in November 1991, Masur announced Johnson's appointment and a rearrangement of the seating of the orchestra. The double bass section would be placed across the back of the hall and wooden baffles added at the sides of the stage to provide a temporary cushion for the brass sound. Masur considered these temporary fixes while everyone awaited Russell Johnson's final recommendations.[56] At the same time, Masur praised the hall, calling it "very beautiful and . . . absolutely OK. The problem was for us on stage."[57]

In the spring of 1992, Russell Johnson submitted his report, citing a severe problem that had to be addressed. He recommended adding four movable ceiling sound reflectors above the stage and four banks of fixed sound reflectors on the sidewalls. After additional discussions, Lincoln Center and the Philharmonic agreed to implement the suggested changes and to have the project overseen by the architect John Burgee. The installation would be done in the three weeks between the end of the Mostly Mozart concerts in August and the Philharmonic's opening night on September 12, 1992.

The two institutions agreed to share the $3 million cost, with Lincoln Center providing two-thirds and the Philharmonic one-third of the total. This reflected the relative use of the hall by the two parties and was consistent with the constituency agreement about allocating capital expenditures.

A few journalists reported that Russell Johnson considered the ceiling diffusers a first stage and that he had suggested raising the ceiling above the stage at a later time. (The Jaffe Acoustics report had suggested raising the ceiling as an option.) Neither Lincoln Center nor the Philharmonic gave credibility to these reports. They suggested that everyone needed to concentrate on the impact of the diffusers.

The critical response to the changes was again favorable. One critic even claimed an improvement in the overall quality of the

The Metropolitan Opera House and North Plaza, Winter 2000.

hall's sound, including the bass reverberance.[58] The musicians reported great improvement in hearing each other from left to right and front to back, although some woodwind players did not notice much change. Most outside observers commented unfavorably on the look of the wooden and glass reflectors but accepted this as the price of improvement.

Throughout his remaining tenure, Kurt Masur continued to fight for the addition of an organ in Avery Fisher Hall, but the success of the onstage changes muted any further Philharmonic pressures.

That issue would become part of the broader set of discussions in the late 1990s between Lincoln Center and the Philharmonic about the possible modernization of Avery Fisher Hall, including changes in the auditorium. With the approval of its landlord, Lincoln Center, the New York Philharmonic engaged the architectural firm Skidmore Owings and Merrill (SOM) to undertake a study of Avery Fisher Hall. The architects estimated it would take between $30 million and $40 million to pay for deferred maintenance items alone. This survey served as the basis for the Avery Fisher Hall portion of the 1999 capital needs assessment of the whole of Lincoln Center by the architects and planners Beyer Blinder Belle.

In March 2002, at the behest of the Constituent Development Program, SOM partner Leigh Breslau presented the firm's analysis of the difficulties confronting Avery Fisher Hall, as well as recommendations and cost estimates for their remediation. Two possible scenarios eventually emerged: a new hall that would expand outward from its existing footprint, or a renovated hall that would expand upward within its existing envelope. (Given the estimated costs associated with either of those options at the time, some people even suggested blowing up the hall altogether and beginning anew.) The general consensus was that expanding outside the existing footprint would be preferable if the money could be raised. In either case, the New York Philharmonic (and Lincoln Center's own ongoing programming efforts in the hall, such as Mostly Mozart and

Great Performers) would be displaced while work on Avery Fisher Hall was completed, a costly and inconvenient consequence.

In June 2002, having invited eight architects to submit plans for the hall's redevelopment, Lincoln Center and the New York Philharmonic announced three finalists: Sir Norman Foster, Rafael Moneo, and the team of Richard Meier and Arata Isozaki. Foster, known for his work at the British Museum in London and Berlin's Reichstag, was selected in early 2003, although a decision had yet to be made on which option would ultimately be selected. The Philharmonic and Lincoln Center, meanwhile, explored the pros and cons, as well as the estimated cost, of these alternatives ($465 million for a hall with an expanded envelope; $305 million for a renovated hall within the existing four walls). What was not generally known at Lincoln Center was that the Philharmonic was also investigating an additional option: a possible permanent move to Carnegie Hall, which the orchestra believed would cost far less.

Work was proceeding on vetting these options when the New York Philharmonic suddenly and startlingly announced that it was entering into discussions with Carnegie Hall to form a single musical performing arts institution. A joint statement issued on June 2, 2003, by New York Philharmonic chairman Paul B. Guenther and Carnegie Hall chairman Sanford I. Weill said, "The merger of the 161-year-old New York Philharmonic and the 112-year-old Carnegie Hall will create an institution of unmatched potential."[59] The orchestra, in the process, would abandon Lincoln Center—and the large capital campaign it would have to undertake to pay for the work on Avery Fisher Hall. News of the potential deal was leaked prematurely to the *New York Times*, which published it on May 31, two days after the Philharmonic had informed Lincoln Center that redevelopment of Avery Fisher Hall was no longer its leading option.

The announcement surprised many, and angered some, who felt it a betrayal of the original Lincoln Center concept. By midsummer, however, what had seemed like a done deal was beginning to look less secure. While Lincoln Center and the New York Philharmonic wrangled over legal issues having to do with the orchestra's potential abrogation of its Avery Fisher Hall lease, the orchestra examined more closely the pros and cons of a merger versus simple tenancy at Carnegie Hall. Either way, the orchestra was insisting on artistic primacy in Carnegie Hall, and negotiations began to falter. On October 7, 2003, the New York Philharmonic announced that it was abandoning its plans to move, citing "irresolvable conflicts over which organization would dominate performance time."[60] Carnegie Hall had not been willing to give the Philharmonic priority in its use of the hall, and, for its part, the orchestra was not willing to be just one tenant among many at Carnegie Hall.

The Philharmonic returned to Lincoln Center as Avery Fisher Hall's primary tenant, an arrangement it had enjoyed since the opening of the hall in 1962. "Welcome home," Center president Reynold Levy was quoted as saying. "All is forgiven. We have a lot to discuss."[61]

The single biggest need, according to chairman Bruce Crawford, was to forge a better working relationship between Lincoln Center and the Philharmonic, one that acknowledged the difficulties inherent in sharing a hall. "The net result," he said, "is that we both recognized our mutual stake in the financial success of the hall and have found ways to improve that."[62]

But the substantial and real problems of the hall remained. In welcoming the Philharmonic back into the Lincoln Center family, management assured the orchestra that all would work together to find a satisfactory solution. In June 2004, Lincoln Center and the Philharmonic conducted an experiment where several front rows of seats were removed and the stage was brought forward. The results were encouraging, and Norman Foster was asked to do a feasibility study based on this new option for Avery Fisher Hall: redoing the hall with the stage brought forward, and reorganizing and improving the hall's public areas and back-of-house spaces. Subsequent to that, Mostly Mozart used the same configuration in 2005. Detailed renovation options for Avery Fisher Hall are still under review as of June 2006.

The Visual Arts

> I feel strongly that the performing arts and the arts in general have not been recognized for the important role they play in the lives of human beings. There is a fundamental love of music and dance and the visual arts among people. It's a part of human nature.
>
> —AMYAS AMES, THE CHAIRMAN OF LINCOLN CENTER 1970–1981

The original incorporators of Lincoln Center believed that the visual arts not only would enhance the physical plant but would also envelop visitors in a more complete aesthetic experience. Mindful of this, the board in 1961 invited Frank Stanton—the then president of CBS, a Lincoln Center board member, and a modern art connoisseur—to chair the newly created Arts & Acquisitions Committee, which would establish criteria for works of art to be accepted as gifts or commissioned by Lincoln Center. Together with the Center's architects, the committee—which included Stanton; René d'Harnoncourt, the director of the Museum of Modern Art; and Andrew Ritchie, the director of the Yale University Art Gallery—determined which works would be installed in the Center's buildings and public spaces. "Whatever went in had to meet the overall concept of the design of the Center, as envisioned by the group of architects involved and the art committee,"[63] recalled Thaddeus Crapster, an architect and a onetime assistant director of construction at Lincoln Center. (A detailed accounting of how the initial major works of art were selected appears in chapter 14 of Edgar B. Young's *Lincoln Center: The Building of an Institution*.[64] These included Henry Moore's *Reclining Figure*, Alexander Calder's *Le Guichet*, Elie Nadelman's *Circus Women* and *Two Female Nudes* in the New York State Theater, and Richard Lippold's *Orpheus and Apollo* in Philharmonic Hall.)

One of the Center's most noteworthy and enduring programs—known officially as the Lincoln Center/List Poster and Print

Artist Larry Rivers with Vera List, who, with her husband, Albert A. List, established the Lincoln Center/List Poster and Print Program, which published its first poster and print in 1962.

Program—took shape in those early years. When John D. Rockefeller 3rd first approached Albert A. List for a financial contribution to the construction of Lincoln Center, List's wife, Vera, suggested they do something in addition to contributing to "bricks and mortar." She proposed a program that would invite contemporary artists to create posters and prints to complement special events, openings, and performances at Lincoln Center. Mrs. List greatly admired the graphic arts, with which she and her husband had become familiar on their European travels, and she understood their public relations potential. "I came up with the idea of the posters because I used to go to Carnegie Hall, and the only thing they had there were the large three-sheeters, with everything just written out about what was in the offing. My thought was that posters that had an image would better catch the public's attention. And it would bring the artists' created images to the public."[65]

With the full approval of the Arts & Acquisitions Committee, Vera List established a program whose original goal was to provide fine art commemorative announcements and to make those posters and prints financially accessible to the general public.[66] Vera List maintained a strong hand in selecting the artists, each of whom was invited to create an image that would then be produced in two versions: as a signed print and as a poster. The artist Ben Shahn was invited to design the first List print and poster, commemorating the 1962 opening of Philharmonic Hall.

In 1972, Mrs. List asked Delmar Hendricks—the booking manager for Philharmonic Hall and Alice Tully Hall and a man with a strong affinity for the graphic arts—to assume responsibility for the program, which had been run off-site through the HLK Gallery in Boston. The gallery, according to Hendricks, "had had great sway in commissioning the artists. Lincoln Center did the contracts but usually followed the advice of the Boston dealers. Printing was done in New York. The prints, which were signed and numbered by the artist in a limited run, were shipped to Boston for sale, while the posters remained in New York for sale at Lincoln Center."[67]

Hendricks, realizing that HLK kept a significant percentage of each print sale, proposed an alternate arrangement. "I went to Vera and said that we had to consider reorganizing this system . . . with me doing the selling," he remembered.[68] Mrs. List readily agreed, and, with Lincoln Center's backing, Hendricks began to run the program—including the sale of both the prints and the posters—from a specially outfitted office in the old CBS broadcast room of Avery Fisher Hall.

Hendricks and Mrs. List "visited galleries, looking for something that excited us. The majority of the time, we found we liked something abstract," Hendricks recalled.[69] Artists invited to participate in the early days included Robert Indiana (for the opening of the New York State Theater in 1964) and Andy Warhol (for the 1967 New York Film Festival). Later, Mrs. List added younger artists who were then lesser known, such as Nancy Graves, Sol LeWitt, and Elizabeth Murray. Most of the major art movements of the previous fifty years—including Ab Ex, Pop Art, and Minimalism—were represented. By the end of 2006, the collection consisted of 160 different images.

"It's not only the outstanding artists who have been selected over the years, but the quality of production is amazing. These are posters made the way posters were at the beginning of the twentieth century. . . . They are silk-screened, and there's a lot of handwork in them,"[70] said Thomas Lollar, the List Poster and Print Program's director since 1997. "All List prints and posters are produced under the supervision of the artist and are made by printmakers who are masters of their craft."[71] The prints, which carry no typography, are signed and numbered by the artist; the less-expensive poster versions feature both the artwork and the typography announcing the event for which the artwork was produced. A truly outstanding collection, the List prints and posters blend the visual and the performing arts in a memorable way. Selections from the collection have been exhibited in the United States and abroad and are included in the collections of many museums, including the Metropolitan Museum of Art and the Museum of Modern Art.

The List Poster and Print Program proved to be not only an effective public-relations tool but a self-sustaining financial effort as well, fulfilling Mrs. List's original goals. "I believe very strongly in the visual arts," she once said, "and having them be an essential part of what goes on at Lincoln Center."[72]

The Arts & Acquisitions Committee, so active in the selection of works of art in the early days of the Center, eventually evolved into a group that met on an "as needed" basis. One of its main functions was to oversee the physical condition of the artworks, primarily sculpture, on display at Lincoln Center. These included the three outdoor pieces—Alexander Calder's *Le Guichet*, Henry Moore's *Reclining Figure*, and Yaacov Agam's *Three x Three Interplay*—and other works installed inside each building on campus. While almost all of these are owned by Lincoln Center, the responsibility for their maintenance belongs to the resident organization in whose facility the work resides.

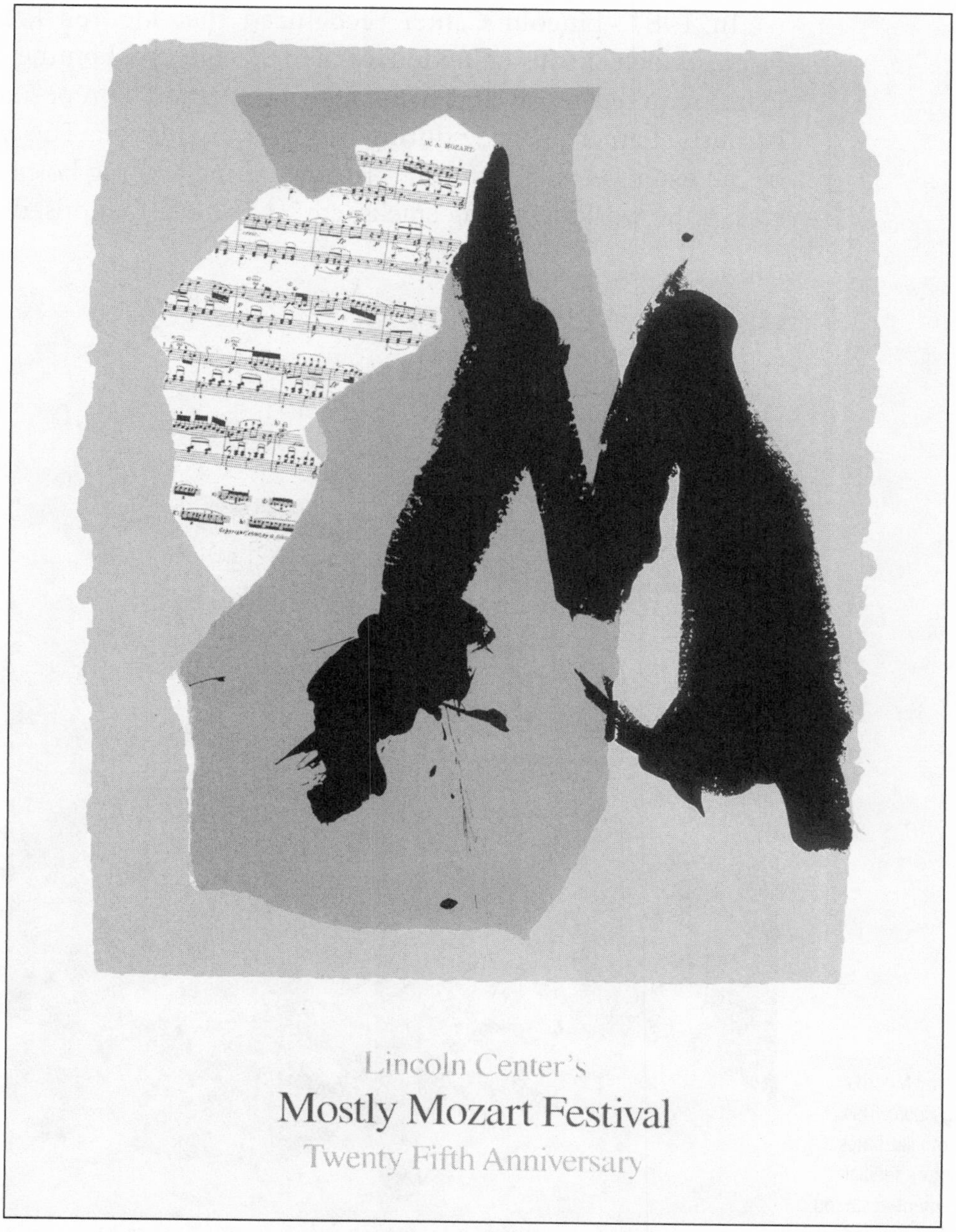

Artist Robert Motherwell's 1991 Mostly Mozart Festival poster, commemorating the festival's twenty-fifth anniversary.

In 1981, Lincoln Center recognized that Moore's *Reclining Figure*, which sits in the middle of the reflecting pool on the North Plaza, required repair and restoration in addition to repositioning because of an error made during its initial installation. This was to be "an extensive job" requiring "rigging, lifting, cutting holes in the side of the work, repairing cracks, etc."[73] The artist, apprised of the

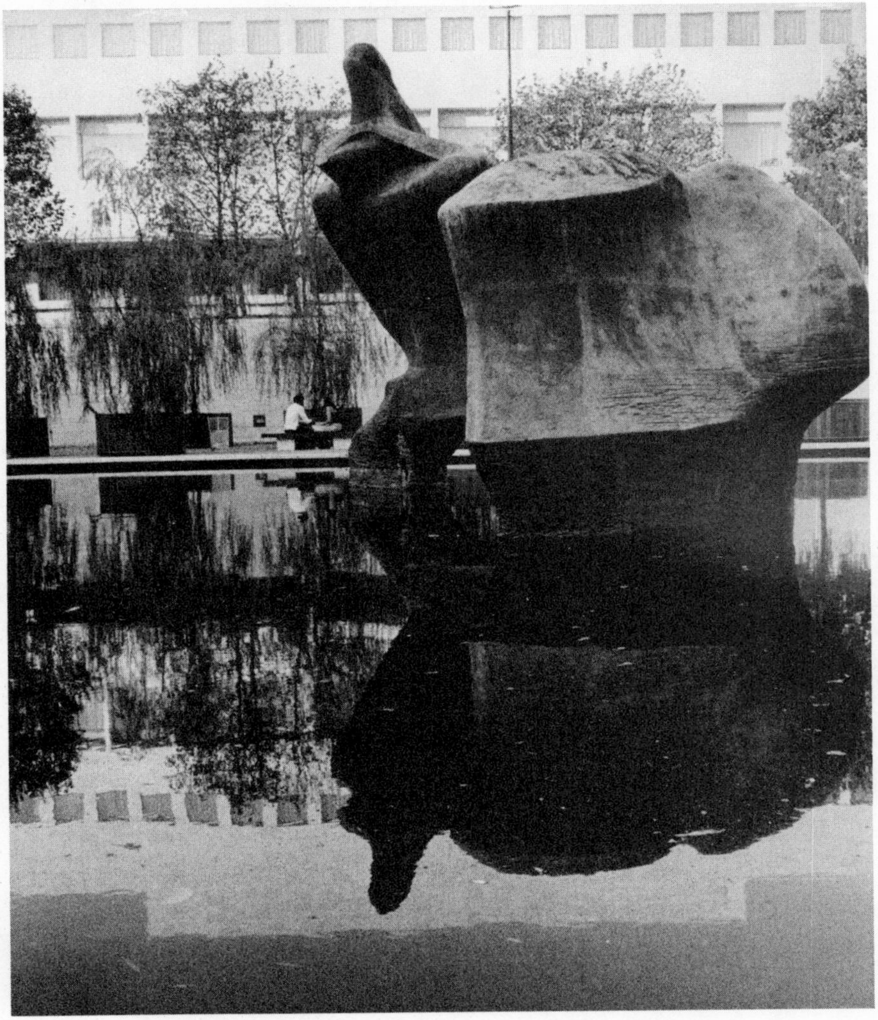

Artist Henry Moore's *Reclining Figure*. This 1974 photo illustrates the sculpture's initial misplacement—it sat too high in the reflecting pool. This was later corrected.

plans, gave his approval. Gordon Bunshaft, the architect of the New York Library for the Performing Arts building that overlooks the *Reclining Figure* and a close personal friend of Henry Moore, invited Lincoln Center chairman Martin E. Segal to accompany him on a visit to the sculptor's studio outside London. Moore queried Bunshaft and Segal about the planned restoration and what it would cost. Soon thereafter, Lincoln Center received a generous gift of £100,000 pounds from the Henry Moore Foundation to underwrite the repairs and the repositioning.[74] Segal cited Lincoln Center president John Mazzola, who had kept Moore advised about possible problems with his sculpture's installation in the earlier years, for his important role in arranging the 1981 discussion with Moore and the artist's subsequent gift. Work on the sculpture and the reflecting pool was completed in 1983, wrote one observer, "enabling New Yorkers to see the figure as originally conceived for the first time."[75]

In 1995, the Arts & Acquisitions Committee retained Christine Roussel, Inc., to assess the condition of its collection. Roussel found that many of the works on display at Lincoln Center needed attention, with Jasper Johns's *Numbers, 1964*, located in the New York State Theater, requiring the most.[76] Lincoln Center subsequently contracted Roussel to perform the necessary restoration and maintenance of its outdoor pieces, as well as of works in Avery Fisher Hall, the Juilliard School, and Alice Tully Hall. By the end of 1997, most of this work had been completed. In addition, Lincoln Center agreed to make an interest-free loan to City Center to pay for artwork restoration in the New York State Theater, which City Center otherwise would have been financially unable to undertake.[77] (Ultimately, *Numbers, 1964*, was judged too fragile and costly to be restored.)

Many of the twenty-eight works in Lincoln Center's collection have appreciated significantly in value over the years. One difficult issue that any substantial collection imposes upon its guardian is the frequently controversial possibility of de-accessioning a work of art. The assessed value of one work in the Center's collection—Jasper

Johns's painting *Numbers, 1964*, which Lincoln Center had commissioned specifically for the New York State Theater at Philip Johnson's suggestion, using funds provided by Albert and Vera List—had soared. When Lincoln Center was approached by a potential buyer of the painting, the board of directors, believing it had a fiduciary obligation to consider multimillion-dollar offers, authorized its executive committee to decide "whether and, if so, on what terms such a sale should be made."[78] News of the deliberations was met with some negative criticism in the press and serious opposition among leading figures in the art world. At a special meeting on January 25, 1999, the board voted not to pursue the matter.

The Lincoln Center collection (for a full accounting of the collection, see *Painting and Sculpture at Lincoln Center*, a Lincoln Center publication compiled during George Weissman's chairmanship) remained static for many years, with three notable exceptions. Jean Lipman, with her husband, Howard, had made several important gifts of art to Lincoln Center, including Calder's *Le Guichet* in 1965. When she died, her son and her daughter-in-law donated the maquette for Richard Lippold's sculpture *Orpheus and Apollo* that hangs in Avery Fisher Hall.[79] The maquette was installed in 1999 in a specially designed exhibition space carved out of the wall on the first tier level of Avery Fisher Hall.

In 1995, Lincoln Center, the Chamber Music Society, and the Juilliard School commissioned the artist Leonard Baskin to create a bronze relief of the composer William Schuman, Lincoln Center's president from 1962 to 1968. The relief was installed in Alice Tully Hall in early 1996.[80] That same year, the Arts & Acquisitions Committee, and subsequently the Executive Committee of the board of Lincoln Center, approved commissioning a large clock sculpture, to be designed by the architect Philip Johnson and donated, maintained, and sponsored by Movado. The clock sculpture, initially slated for installation on the Josie Robertson Plaza, was envisioned, according to Mr. Johnson, as "an inverted asymmetrical slab . . . a new kind of architecture defiant of geometry."[81]

The project received all necessary approvals but met opposition among some constituents and Lincoln Center board members regarding its intended placement. Lincoln Center then chose an alternative site across Columbus Avenue in Dante Park, where the work, *TimeSculpture*, would be visible both to Lincoln Center audiences and to the public at large. It was installed there in 1999.

Because its campus offers a perfect venue for outdoor sculpture, Lincoln Center has from time to time mounted temporary installations organized by other institutions. For instance, during the summer of 1999, it displayed several works from the Empire State Plaza collection. During the summer of 2004, *Franz West: Recent Sculpture*, an exhibition of seven large-scale lacquered aluminum sculptures, was installed on Broadway at the entrance to the Josie Robertson Plaza. The exhibition was the first in what was hoped would be a continuing collaborative effort between Lincoln Center and the Public Art Fund, which produces innovative exhibitions of contemporary art throughout New York City. Lincoln Center management welcomed the exhibition as "an amenity for campus audiences and as an attraction to bring people to the campus"[82] during July and August, when its rich and varied summer programming draws patrons and visitors from all over the world.

The visual arts are an integral part of the Lincoln Center experience. Posters recalling many of the Center's hallmark events hang strategically at various spots on campus. Around almost any corner, both within the halls and outside on the plazas, the concertgoer, the theatergoer, the ballet aficionado, the opera lover, and the casual stroller can encounter a wonderful work of art from the Center's fine collection. These surprise, please, and stimulate visitors to Lincoln Center, where the performing and the visual arts so richly complement each other.

4

MAKING THINGS HAPPEN

Leadership at Lincoln Center

LINCOLN CENTER HAS ALWAYS RELIED ON STRONG LEADERSHIP to help make things happen. John D. Rockefeller 3rd served first as president and then as chairman between 1956 and 1970, during which time the Center was conceived and built. The vision of William Schuman, the president from 1962 to 1968, did much to set the stage for future programming initiatives. Those who followed these two Lincoln Center pioneers continued to steer a steady course for the institution and also widened its reach in so many important ways.

Amyas Ames, chairman of Lincoln Center from 1970 to 1981.

John Mazzola, managing director, then president, of Lincoln Center from 1970 to1982.

Amyas Ames, 1970–1981

On May 11, 1970, the Lincoln Center board of directors unanimously elected Amyas Ames as its new chairman. Ames had played a leading role in the institution's management for many years as a board member, as president and chairman of the Philharmonic, and as chairman of the Center's executive committee. Although not a member of the original group that had conceived the idea of a "musical arts center" in the mid-1950s, Ames had not been far behind. He joined the Center's board in 1963 and worked closely with founding chairman John D. Rockefeller 3rd for most of the 1960s to complete the physical construction of Lincoln Center. Ames then collaborated closely with Rockefeller and others in the equally demanding effort to place its operations on a sensible administrative basis and a sound financial foundation. He was the logical successor to Rockefeller, not least because the constituents admired him and felt comfortable with him, believing that he understood their needs and would champion their interests.

Serving with Ames was John Mazzola, the executive vice president and general manager in charge of day-to-day operations. Mazzola also had a long history at Lincoln Center. His law firm—Milbank, Tweed—had assigned him to handle the Center's legal affairs on a part-time basis in 1962, and Mazzola became a permanent member of the Center's staff a year later. After William Schuman's resignation in December 1968, he was designated chief executive officer[1] (with title changes to managing director in 1970 and president in 1977).

The Ames-Mazzola partnership succeeded despite, or perhaps because of, the fact that they had such different personalities.

Ames was a senior partner in Kidder, Peabody & Company, one of Wall Street's oldest and most respected investment banking firms. Tall, elegant, and always impeccably dressed, Ames was somewhat reserved. An experienced investor, he had been a strong advocate of responsible financial management during his years on the Center's board.

Mazzola was a gregarious presence who actually enjoyed the many social events he was required to attend. He and his wife, Sylvia, were well known in the theater and visual arts worlds, and they frequently represented Lincoln Center in this broader community. Mazzola's skill and legal training helped Ames to bridge differences within the Lincoln Center family.

Ames and Mazzola faced two critical problems: repairing the strained relations with most, if not all, of the resident organizations and closing the yawning financial deficit. Failure to deal effectively with either issue could threaten the effectiveness of Lincoln Center.

In regard to relationships between Lincoln Center and its constituents, Ames and Mazzola had to tread cautiously. By and large, the resident organizations believed that the Center had been built for them. At the same time, many Lincoln Center board members, while wary of deepening the institution's financial problems, felt that the Center should be more than just a real-estate corporation, a holding company, or a central administrative expression of the constituents. It could also be—and, in fact, had proved to be during the mid- and late-1960s—a powerful and innovative programming force in the performing arts.[2] Ames walked a fine line between these views. "I believed that the constituent art companies were what Lincoln Center was all about—that its grandeur, its bricks and mortar were wholly secondary to the art companies that gave birth to it. I also believed separate programming of Lincoln Center, Inc., was only desirable when it was helpful to and not conflicting with the constituents."[3]

Ames pursued a balanced course throughout his tenure. While he and Mazzola helped to repair the frayed relations with the constituents, they also pursued independent programming initiatives on behalf of Lincoln Center. The decision to proceed with *Live from Lincoln Center* provided an excellent example. The televised series, aired first in 1976, soon made Lincoln Center a household name around the country. As an additional benefit, from the beginning, Lincoln Center wisely provided a fee to each constituent appearing on *Live from Lincoln Center*.

Under Ames, the Center's own programming actually broadened, as some of William Schuman's artistic initiatives matured. The Chamber Music Society achieved constituent status at Lincoln Center in 1972, followed by the Film Society in 1974. In the politically turbulent early 1970s, the Center initiated its community programming efforts, and by 1974 Lincoln Center Out of Doors had become a fixture each summer. Other seeds planted by Schuman led to the official creation in 1975 of the Lincoln Center Institute, the Center's major educational effort.

Lincoln Center's precarious financial situation hampered new programming initiatives for a time, at least on the scale envisioned by Schuman. By 1968, the Center's undesignated reserve fund had dwindled to barely $500,000 as expenses overwhelmed income. In fact, by mid-October the budgetary situation had deteriorated to the point that technical bankruptcy by year's end was a strong possibility. As Edgar B. Young observed, "Lincoln Center was not merely in a period of retrenchment, it was in a battle for survival."[4]

Rockefeller, Ames, Mazzola, and other members of Lincoln Center's board dealt with the crisis by rigorously cutting staff and other expenditures—actions that reduced the operating budget by more than 60 percent and brought the situation under temporary control. More important, the board decided that management had to base Lincoln Center's future operating budgets on rigorous estimates of actual costs and realistic revenue streams, and to subject future programming initiatives, such as Schuman's innovative summer programs, to the same strict standard.

For Lincoln Center's staff and board, the financial crisis would remain a vivid presence for years to come. Thus, when Ames took the helm in mid-1970, one of his principal tasks was rebuilding the Center's financial resources so that it could again play the role intended for it by the founders. This was not an easy undertaking, and Ames and Mazzola helped the board in developing a multipronged approach to deal with its strategies to increase governmental assistance and annual giving from corporations, foundations, and individuals, as well as an effort to rebuild the endowment.

It was understood that Lincoln Center would never have been created without significant financial support from the federal government, New York State, and New York City, but Ames and Mazzola realized that the arts deserved greater government support on the operational level as well, and this is where they focused their efforts. At a time when public support for the arts was in its infancy, Ames threw himself into a very public role by chairing both the New York State Concerned Citizens for the Arts and the National Partnership for the Arts. "Such organized lobbying was completely new for the arts and resulted in meaningful support for all the arts for the first time from both our state and federal governments," Ames later wrote.[5] His public lobbying efforts drew praise from Ames's friend C. Douglas Dillon: "I can only say you are a wizard as well as a wonderful citizen."[6] Ames's efforts bore fruit as both federal and state support for the arts in general and for Lincoln Center in particular increased during the 1970s.

Ames also took the lead in persuading the constituents to merge their individual fund-raising efforts with corporations by establishing a joint outreach to New York's business community, although Lincoln Center itself would be only one beneficiary. The Consolidated Corporate Fund Drive—headed by Hoyt Ammidon, a Lincoln Center board member and the chairman of the United States Trust

Company—replaced the individual constituent appeals to the business community and, the *New York Times* reported, "was meant to have a great wallop."[7] The money raised was apportioned to Lincoln Center and its constituents, and the fund drive proved to be an early example of successful cooperation within the context of the Center.

Ames understood that Lincoln Center's financial stability required a substantial increase in its small endowment. This was never an easy objective to achieve, since donors preferred to contribute to almost anything other than maintenance. Fortunately, a $10 million bequest in early 1971 from the estate of Martha Baird Rockefeller—the widow of John D. Rockefeller Jr. and a concert pianist in her younger days—restored the Center's reserves to a respectable level and eased operational concerns, at least for a time. The Edna McConnell Clark Foundation provided $4.4 million later that same year as an endowment to support the Center's educational programs.

In 1979, with the leadership of board member Lawrence Wien and others, a Lincoln Center Fund campaign was initiated, with a goal of $20 million in new gifts. One unique aspect of this capital campaign was the tactic of seeking "partnership" contributions of at least $100,000 from individuals, foundations, and corporations.

The Lincoln Center Fund campaign coincided with other constituent campaigns, most notably the $100 million Metropolitan Opera drive. This and the continuing appeals to corporations by the Consolidated Corporate Fund Drive led to soul-searching about the potential conflicts and confusion, especially with corporate donors. By the late 1970s, however, the resident companies had found ways to approach corporations for special projects on top of what each corporation might be contributing to the Consolidated Corporate Fund Drive. This coincided with an increased emphasis by corporations on marketing-driven contributions and the resulting desire for more public recognition of such gifts.

These initiatives generated substantial new money for the Center and improved its overall financial situation. In fiscal year 1981, the Center raised $7 million from all sources, including annual support for its programming activities and *Live from Lincoln Center*. At the same time, the Consolidated Corporate Fund Drive had almost reached its goal of $3 million.[8] This was a substantial change from the precarious situation of a decade earlier.

Avery Fisher, the retired head of Fisher Radio, deserved recognition for the brighter financial picture. His unsolicited $10 million gift in 1973—at that time, the largest single donation Lincoln Center had ever received—provided an operating endowment for the renamed Avery Fisher Hall and also supported the Avery Fisher Artist Program, which included the Avery Fisher Prize and Avery Fisher Career Grants. These gave special recognition and assistance to talented young instrumentalists. "Musicians of outstanding ability are such an important part of our culture," Mr. Fisher said. "But they are like flowers that must bloom at a particular time. They have to be helped at the right moments."[9] In 1976, much of the remaining gift was used to redo the acoustics and the auditorium of Avery Fisher Hall.

Even though Lincoln Center continued to run a substantial deficit (about $800,000 in 1979–1980), its invigorated fund-raising capacity became a base for future progress toward eliminating the deficit.

Amyas Ames believed that the resident companies were the heart and soul of Lincoln Center.[10] Yet he also had a clear appreciation for the umbrella organization of Lincoln Center, Inc., and the ways in which it benefited the member constituents: its organized lobbying for government support of the arts; its ability to raise funds in which all could share; and its ability to reach audiences around the country with what the member companies had to offer through *Live from Lincoln Center*.

Upon Ames's 1981 retirement, the *New York Times* wrote of him: he "thought of himself primarily as a caretaker for its constituent members—the New York Philharmonic, the Metropolitan

Opera, New York City Opera, New York City Ballet, the Juilliard School, the Chamber Music Society of Lincoln Center, Lincoln Center Theater, and the Film Society of Lincoln Center. Mr. Ames can be called the constituent chairman."[11] In retrospect, it was clear that his impact on the institution was far greater than that. Ames had restored the constituents' belief in the project and reestablished the basis for the Center to play an essential, if more measured, role in the future.

Martin E. Segal, 1981–1986

Although Ames had done much to first stabilize and then strengthen Lincoln Center's finances and to place its management on a somewhat sounder administrative basis, his successor, Martin E. Segal, faced several major challenges when he assumed the chairmanship in June 1981. One of the most serious of these was the Lincoln Center Theater, the very existence of which was in doubt. In addition, Lincoln Center's finances remained in a precarious condition. Many of the halls had operated in the red for years, the gift shops continued to lose money, and an effective accounting system had not yet been implemented to deal with the serious delays in billings for halls and other problems. Moreover, Segal and the board confronted the consequences of deferred maintenance. The New York State Theater desperately needed renovation, as did much of the Center's aging campus, particularly the walkways and the plazas.

Martin E. Segal, chairman of Lincoln Center from 1981 to 1986.

Segal had the right set of skills and leadership qualities to take on these challenges. An immigrant who arrived in the United States from Russia at age five, he had established his own consulting and actuarial company in 1939 and built it into a successful national enterprise. After arranging for the sale of his company in 1978, he devoted increasing time to the investment-banking firm Wertheim and Co. All during his business career, Segal had established a reputation for probity and meticulous attention to detail.

While still active in business, Segal became involved with a number of cultural and civic institutions. He served on the city's Board of Hospitals when Robert F. Wagner Jr. was mayor. At the request of Mayor John V. Lindsay in 1971, Segal played an important role in steering the City Center of Music and Drama—the umbrella organization for the New York City Ballet and the New York City Opera—through its rough waters in the mid-1970s. He then served as the first chairman of the Commission for Cultural Affairs from 1975 to 1977 in Mayor Abraham Beame's administration. The fresh red rose Segal always wore pinned to the lapel of an immaculately tailored suit easily identified him around town.

Segal believed that part of his job as chairman of Lincoln Center would be to influence national arts policy. In particular, he thought governments at all levels should support the arts financially and in other ways, and he fought against the first Reagan administration's proposed cuts in the federal arts budget. In addition, he announced his desire to make New York once again the home of an international summer festival and to encourage Lincoln Center to expand its role in television.[12]

After Segal became chairman, he and John Mazzola increasingly found themselves in disagreement as they dealt with difficult issues, including the seeming inability of management to eliminate persistent accounting problems. In late August 1982, Segal and Mazzola agreed that Mazzola would leave his position as president at the end of the year while remaining as a consultant through 1983. In response to press speculation about the reasons for Mazzola's retirement, Segal referred to the former president's "real contribution" to Lincoln Center over twenty years and called him a "highly intelligent and imaginative administrator."[13]

In March 1983, the search committee recommended Glenn W. Ferguson, a former diplomat and the head of Radio Free Europe, as the new president. While the board ratified the choice, Segal and other board members soon questioned Ferguson's suitability. In December of the same year, Ferguson resigned in order to "pursue the career objectives with which I was associated before coming to the Center."[14]

A new search quickly focused on Nathan Leventhal for the position. As deputy mayor for operations in Edward I. Koch's administration, Leventhal had demonstrated a sure grasp of both management and politics as the city struggled with a new "era of limitations" in the aftermath of the 1970s fiscal crisis. A lawyer by profession, Leventhal had served as Mayor John V. Lindsay's chief of staff in the early 1970s and then as chief counsel for Senator Edward M. Kennedy's Subcommittee on Administrative Practices and Procedures. Segal knew him well and enthusiastically endorsed the search committee's nomination of Leventhal as president and chief operating officer in March 1984.

Nathan Leventhal, president of Lincoln Center from 1984 to 2000.

Even before Leventhal's arrival, Segal and Lincoln Center's management team had made considerable progress in transforming the Center's chronic operating deficit into a surplus. The most significant step involved a policy change in the rental of Avery Fisher Hall and Alice Tully Hall. Segal and a majority of the board insisted that these facilities would now have to operate on at least a break-even basis. Much of the fund-raising success of the late 1970s had been used to cover the annual deficits of the two halls. (More than $2 million had been transferred from the Lincoln Center Fund in the four years ending 1981–1982 for this purpose, and additional funds in the form of realized capital gains had been moved from the endowment for their capital improvement and maintenance.)

From Segal's perspective, this situation had to end. Gently but firmly, he negotiated increases in rental fees, despite considerable resistance from the resident organizations that used the two halls. The goal was to reduce their deficits by at least 50 percent over a five-year period and then to eliminate them entirely. Lincoln Center would no longer subsidize the halls with transfers from its own endowment.

In late 1981, the Lincoln Center board gave its final approval to a new fund established by the founders of *Reader's Digest*, DeWitt and Lila Acheson Wallace, to support new productions and commissions by some of Lincoln Center's constituents. The Lila Acheson and DeWitt Wallace Fund for Lincoln Center was to be managed independently, and a number of board members expressed reluctance at lending the Center's name to an institution they did not control. Another concern was the preponderance of *Reader's Digest* stock, which was not publicly traded, in the fund's portfolio. There was also grumbling over the fact that some constituents and Lincoln Center itself would not benefit from it; however, because the income would go a long way toward stabilizing the operations of its beneficiary constituents, the board agreed to the relationship. The decision to accept the Wallace proposal proved to be more important than anyone could have realized at the time. Eventually, the Wallace Fund for Lincoln Center was dissolved, the *Reader's Digest* stock was sold, and the proceeds were distributed as Wallace Endowments to each qualifying constituent. This had a major positive impact on the finances of the constituent beneficiaries.

As already noted in chapter 3, the process that would lead to Lincoln Center's expansion through the construction of the Rose Building had begun in the last months of Amyas Ames's tenure. Martin E. Segal moved it forward energetically. In addition to committing Lincoln Center to this essential expansion and strengthening its finances and fund-raising, Segal also helped to resolve the difficult

Lincoln Center Theater issue. He took the lead in insisting on changes in the Vivian Beaumont's board and artistic leadership, which ultimately led to the theater becoming one of the Center's most successful constituents.

Segal also planned for the coming decades. In 1984, he established the Committee on the Future, chaired by RCA chairman and CEO Thornton F. Bradshaw, to consider the many challenges facing Lincoln Center and to propose ways of meeting them. The committee's report stressed the importance of maintaining open, healthy, and constructive relationships among all of Lincoln Center's constituents and called for greater emphasis on arts education and renewing the subscriber audience base through concerted and better-conducted marketing efforts. The committee commended the significant improvement in the Center's financial condition but warned "that financial results are vulnerable to even small declines in audience attendance" and noted that Lincoln Center was "becoming more dependent on the generosity of a limited set of financial contributors."[15]

The Committee on the Future also debated whether Lincoln Center and its constituents should continue to serve "a public that is interested in the art forms of its existing constituents" or should expand to include other art forms.[16] The report concluded that "for the time being, Lincoln Center should focus on excellence in its core offerings and that no compelling case can be made for adding a new constituent in an area like jazz."[17]

Segal's years as chairman were marked by steady and substantial progress. The financial situation, in particular, had been transformed during his five years at the helm, which ended in June 1986. With the able assistance of staff and board members, the $313,000 operating deficit in 1981 turned into a $903,000 surplus by 1985.

A number of factors contributed to this happy result: the endowment had more than doubled to $23.8 million by 1986, contributions for the support of programming and outreach activities had increased, and departmental operating deficits had decreased substantially. In addition, increased hall-rental rates greatly improved the bottom line. A study of the deficit-producing gift shop, spearheaded by then Lincoln Center director Louis V. Gerstner Jr., resulted in the transfer of the management of the shop to the Metropolitan Opera Guild, which subsequently contributed positively to the improved bottom line.[18] In addition, the Center's Consolidated Corporate Fund Drive accounted for a substantial increase in donations. A Chairman's Council designation for certain categories of donors was created, offering special privileges to encourage "a more personal involvement" in Lincoln Center among donors.[19]

Moreover, the continued success of *Live from Lincoln Center*, Great Performers, and Mostly Mozart—all undertakings of Lincoln Center, Inc.—not only kept Lincoln Center squarely in the eye and the mind of the public but also added vitality and excitement to the mix of artistic offerings by each of the Center's constituents.

Lincoln Center's directors marked Segal's retirement with a special and very appropriate gift. Without his knowledge, they raised more than $100,000 to establish the Martin E. Segal Awards, to be given annually to young performers within the Lincoln Center complex for further professional study. The first awards, for $4,000 each, were presented in the spring of 1987; ten years later, the award was increased to $5,000 as a consequence of an additional gift to the fund. Each year, two resident companies are chosen on a rotating basis, and each of these selects a young artist to receive the award. Recipients have included the soprano Michelle De Young, the pianist Helen Huang, the choreographer Christopher Wheeldon, the filmmaker Alan Berliner, the Borromeo String Quartet, and the ballerina Abi Stafford.

Nathan Leventhal captured the essence of these awards for both the young artists and Martin Segal: "Now there is a tribute to Marty that will last beyond an evening in his honor—a gift that is tangible evidence of his love and respect for young people and education, given by a board that has been fortunate to serve with him over the last five years."[20]

George Weissman, 1986–1994

When George Weissman succeeded Martin E. Segal as chairman of Lincoln Center in mid-1986, he brought with him an impressive set of skills and experiences that would stand him in good stead during his tenure. He had been chairman and chief executive officer of Philip Morris, a Fortune 100 company, where he was widely known as a marketing pioneer. Weissman had risen through the corporate ranks as a marketing and advertising executive, and he understood the benefits that would come from strong public relations, as well as a sound balance sheet.

Weissman had also been part of Lincoln Center almost from the beginning. David Ogilvy, the legendary advertising executive, had recruited him in 1959 to work on the initial campaign for Lincoln Center. As part of a volunteer group, Weissman helped to create an intensive national public-relations campaign to make the Center more widely known.[21] "Nothing like it had ever been done before," Weissman remembered, about that 1960 public participation campaign. It succeeded in making the Lincoln Center name a recognizable venue for the arts.[22]

Weissman continued his involvement at Lincoln Center through his work with Martin Segal on the Film Committee, which later became the Film Society of Lincoln Center. In 1972, Weissman was elected to the Lincoln Center board. By that time, he had become a prominent and effective advocate of corporate support for the arts. He would subsequently serve Lincoln Center as a vice chairman of the board and a member of the Committee on the Future.

Weissman had a close working relationship with Nathan Leventhal, Lincoln Center's president. Their personalities and styles complemented each other. Leventhal was a hands-on manager, with detailed knowledge of the budget and operations, who enjoyed Lincoln Center's many cultural offerings, especially the Metropolitan Opera. Weissman was a gregarious and warm presence at Lincoln Center. "George was a tremendously enthusiastic chairman," commented Lincoln Center emeritus board member William F. May. "I never went to an event at Lincoln Center that he wasn't there . . . and he enjoyed it, too."[23]

George Weissman, chairman of Lincoln Center from 1986 to 1994.

Weissman's most immediate concern in 1986 was the fund-raising campaign for the Rose Building, which was successfully concluded in 1990. Weissman delegated day-to-day responsibilities to Leventhal and the Lincoln Center staff, but he actively participated in strategic planning and initiatives and was a strong supporter of the expansion of the Center's year-round programming. A jazz enthusiast, he also played a key role in the formation of the Jazz Department, which eventually became Lincoln Center's twelfth constituent, Jazz at Lincoln Center. "Part of our mission for the future was to experiment," Weissman remarked. "We set up Classical Jazz and Serious Fun! We commissioned something like sixty new works ourselves, and we brought in the Kronos Quartet as part of Great Performers. . . . We did a lot of exciting new things in the programming area."[24] During his tenure, Lincoln Center also introduced its popular Midsummer Night Swing series. To Weissman, "Lincoln Center's playing a much larger role than the landlord it originally started out to be was a very worthwhile thing."[25]

Weissman helped to avert a potential crisis when in 1989 the Exxon Corporation ended its sponsorship of *Live from Lincoln Center* after thirteen years by securing the General Motors Corporation and the Lila Wallace–Reader's Digest Fund as the new sponsors. A grant from the Wallace fund also made possible the educational supplement to the television series *Backstage\Lincoln Center*. Weissman was central in the decision to experiment by putting out in video format nine of the award-winning *Live from Lincoln Center* broadcasts, even though he and the Lincoln Center staff were realistic about the difficulties of marketing such a product.

Weissman's people skills served him well in the ever-tricky area of constituent relations. He patiently worked with all the participating organizations on the construction of the Rose Building and helped to solve a host of issues related to its use. Building on this collaboration, all Lincoln Center constituents joined forces shortly thereafter for the nineteen-month-long 1991–92 Mozart Bicentennial—the first time all the constituents had participated in an "artistic collaboration."[26] Weissman also strongly supported board member Lawrence Wien's 1987 initiative to make the School of American Ballet a full-fledged constituent of Lincoln Center.

At his retirement dinner on October 3, 1994, George Weissman joked about his reputation for fund-raising: "My friends thought there was a mistake on the invitation [which made clear that the event was not a fund-raiser]. For eight years now, I've been twisting arms all over town. I'd call old friends for lunch, and they would say, 'How much will this cost me?'"[27]

Weissman's success as chairman of Lincoln Center rested fundamentally on his commitment to the arts and to Lincoln Center's mission and on his personal qualities, which were described at his retirement as an "easygoing and relaxed attitude combined with the steel that lay underneath."[28] In his eight years of leadership, he left a strong personal stamp on Lincoln Center in many areas.[29]

Beverly Sills, 1994–2002

The election of Beverly Sills as the fifth chairman of Lincoln Center in 1994 represented a series of firsts. Sills, a former diva at the New York City Opera and later the general manager of that company, became the first performing artist to head the Lincoln Center board, and the first woman and the first non–board member to lead the corporation. Sills brought to the job her international celebrity, extensive knowledge of the Lincoln Center complex, awareness of constituent issues, well-honed fund-raising skills, and overall appreciation of the arts.

Sills had retired from the stage in 1980 at age fifty—after a sensational twenty-five-year career—and immediately took over as general manager of the New York City Opera, which she then succeeded in stabilizing and strengthening during her ten years in that post. When approached by Lincoln Center to consider heading its board of directors, Sills embraced the challenge. Her two goals were simple and direct. Since "most of the houses in Lincoln Center are dark from the end of May through the end of September, but the rent, utility bills and salaries still have to be paid," she said, "anything that can be brought in for the summer is in the constituents' benefit. It's time we looked at these big empty theaters and worked with the constituents on ways to fill them."[30] Her second priority was to see children's programming expanded. "Making Lincoln Center less intimidating to them means, as they get into their teens and older, they'll come back again and again. After all, they're our future audience."[31]

As the new chairman (a title she preferred), Sills clearly indicated that she wanted to help shape Lincoln Center's future programming efforts, using her artistic expertise and experience. As she and Nathan Leventhal indicated in a joint interview in early 1996, this led to some initial tension between the two as they sought to define their respective roles.[32] In the same interview, they indicated that they had worked out these differences and had crafted a new and mutually acceptable way of operating—one that welcomed Sills's input in artistic matters, as well

Beverly Sills, chairman of Lincoln Center from 1994 to 2002.

as in fund-raising and official duties while maintaining Leventhal's vital responsibilities as chief operating officer.

Sills and Leventhal soon faced serious constituent opposition to their plan for a Lincoln Center summer arts festival, to open in 1996. They had hoped to use all of Lincoln Center's halls during the summer for what they believed would be a cutting-edge programming initiative that would attract the kind of adventurous audiences that had attended Serious Fun! in previous years.

The constituents objected to the potential competition for fund-raising, especially when the initial budget for the summer festival was reported to be $14 million. Sills managed to reassure the resident organizations that she could raise adequate funding for the festival's first years from sources not likely to give to Lincoln Center for other purposes; however, she and Leventhal scaled back the budget to $8.5 million and agreed to cap total fund-raising at $5.5 million.

The critical success of the 1996 festival and Sills's ability to attract money from new sources eased the constituents' concerns, but the experience led both sides to establish another Chairman's Council, chaired by Sills, to discuss future programming and other issues that might arise between Lincoln Center and the resident organizations. A high point of Sills's tenure was the day in mid-1996 that Jazz at Lincoln Center became an official constituent, the culmination of a long process of incorporating the art form of jazz in Lincoln Center.

Sills proved to be a prodigious fund-raiser. During her tenure, Julian and Josie Robertson donated $25 million to benefit both Lincoln Center and the constituents—at the time, this was the single largest gift from individuals. As a consequence, the Lincoln Center board voted to rename the fountain plaza for Josie Robertson in recognition of this generous and unprecedented contribution. In addition, during Sills's chairmanship, twenty new members were elected to the board, including many individuals to whom Lincoln Center had not previously had access.[33]

Sills and Leventhal were called upon to respond to pressures from the Philharmonic and other resident organizations to modernize the forty-year-old campus. In 1998, management constituted the Committee for the 21st Century to examine Lincoln Center's future needs. At the time, Sills stated that her own priorities for the Center included audience development and bringing the arts to the public schools, as well as some refurbishing and updating of the facilities. The constituents, however, were strongly focused on improving the Center's facilities as the top priority. According to Sills, the next thing she knew, "there was a wish list and an architectural consultant, Beyer Blinder Belle. And the rest is history. It took on a life of its own."[34]

In the midst of these redevelopment discussions, Nathan Leventhal announced in March 2000 that he would leave his post at the end of the year. As the institution's chief operating executive for seventeen years, Leventhal had been an important force in expanding the role of Lincoln Center, Inc., as the successful producer of new programming initiatives and in bringing into being the Center's twelfth constituent, Jazz at Lincoln Center. With the able assistance of his support staff—most particularly, Arlene Shuler, the senior vice president for planning and external affairs; Andre R. Mirabelli, the senior vice president; Robert A. Cappiello, the vice president for finance; and Evelyn M. Finkelstein, his long-time secretary and general counsel—Leventhal successfully managed programs and policy for almost two decades.

In addition, he worked with Frederick P. Rose, Martin E. Segal, and George Weissman in the planning, construction and opening of the Samuel B. and David Rose Building and had contributed to an overall improvement in constituent relations during his tenure.

Sills was surprised by Leventhal's decision and later asserted that she had been contemplating her own retirement and had been preempted by Leventhal's action.[35] Her resignation did not come until two years later.

To replace Leventhal, Lincoln Center turned to one of its own

Gordon Davis, president of Lincoln Center, 2001.

board members, Gordon J. Davis, a real-estate lawyer and former city official in both the Lindsay and the Koch administrations. Davis's enthusiastic participation in many key aspects of completing the Rose Building, his leadership in the creation of Jazz at Lincoln Center as a constituent, and his knowledge of city government and its labyrinth of arcane requirements made him a logical person to head the monumental redevelopment effort. With Beverly Sills's support, he became president of Lincoln Center on January 2001.

During Davis's brief tenure as president, the World Trade Center was destroyed on September 11, 2001. This shocking event stunned New York City into a brief moment of paralysis, and Lincoln Center immediately became a focal point for New Yorkers in search of community and comfort. On September 14, the Josie Robertson Plaza served as the venue for a National Candlelight Remembrance Vigil. Two days later, a special concert at Avery Fisher Hall, "Music and Reflection," featured the Emerson String Quartet and an introduction by Center chairman Beverly Sills. Lincoln Center also played a part in helping to heal a nation on edge. The following Thursday, September 20, Maestro Kurt Masur and the New York Philharmonic—joined by the soprano Heidi Grant Murphy, the baritone Thomas Hampson, the New York Choral Artists, and the American Boychoir—presented a moving performance of Brahms's *A German Requiem*, which was broadcast on *Live from Lincoln Center*.

Twelve firefighters from Engine Company 40/Ladder 35, housed in the Rose Building, were lost in the World Trade Center attack. Lincoln Center made a substantial donation on their behalf to the Uniformed Firefighters Association's Widows and Children's Fund.

Mayor Rudolph Giuliani urged Lincoln Center to resume its regularly scheduled programs and activities, which it did in late

Candlelight vigil on the Josie Robertson Plaza, September 14, 2001, for victims of the World Trade Center attack on September 11, 2001.

September. Every presenting resident organization recognized in a variety of ways the traumatic events of September 11. More than anything else, Lincoln Center's response to the events of that day demonstrated the ability of the arts to touch, comfort, soothe, and ultimately heal both traumatized individuals and a wounded nation.

It had been rumored for some time that Sills and Davis were not getting along, and Davis abruptly resigned on September 27, 2001. In a letter to Sills, he said, "After nine months in this position, it is clear to me, as you and I had discussed, that things are not working out in the way either of us had hoped or expected."[36] Sills responded, "It is with deep and sincere regret that I have accepted your letter of resignation. It has, alas, been a year of so much that has been unexpected and unpredictable."[37]

Janice Price, Lincoln Center's vice president for consumer markets and new technologies, was named interim executive director to assume Davis's duties. In December 2001, Sills announced that she would retire as chairman as soon as a suitable replacement could be found. In January 2002, Price resigned to become head of the new Kimmel Center in Philadelphia. The following month, Lincoln Center announced the appointment of Reynold Levy, the president of the International Rescue Committee, as the next president of Lincoln Center. He assumed his day-to-day duties on May 1, 2002, the same day Sills stepped down as chairman. She was succeeded by Bruce Crawford, the former president and general manager of the Metropolitan Opera and the chairman of Omnicom Group.

Bruce Crawford, 2002–2005

The election of Bruce Crawford as chairman of Lincoln Center in June 2002 came at a particularly propitious moment in the Center's history. Crawford's long involvement with the Metropolitan Opera as general manager (1986–1989) and president of the board (1984–1985 and 1990–1999) afforded him an easy familiarity with the issues confronting Lincoln Center and the vicissitudes of its major players. His leadership abilities and business acumen—as evidenced in his very successful career in advertising, marketing, and communication, most recently as chairman of the board of Omnicom Group, the world's largest advertising and marketing-services company—were to be particularly useful as Lincoln Center planned its redevelopment effort.

Bruce Crawford, chairman of Lincoln Center from 2002 to 2005.

Crawford came to the position of chairman at a difficult time in the Center's history. An economic downturn of considerable depth, constituent in-fighting, and a series of disruptive management changes had all had a detrimental effect on the Center's redevelopment progress. He and Levy made a powerful team, however, each bringing his own considerable talents and temperament to the task at hand.

Crawford's keen intelligence and easy affability served him well in identifying major stumbling blocks, crafting workable compromises, and convincing recalcitrant constituents that there was a greater good to be had by working to overcome differences and thus strengthen the Lincoln Center federation. Levy was known as a consensus-builder with impressive management skills. A lawyer with a Ph.D. in government, and foreign affairs, he also had knowledge of the governmental, foundation, and not-for-profit worlds that would be put to good use at Lincoln Center. Together, they tackled the monumental task of turning Lincoln Center's plans for redevelopment into reality.

Reynold Levy, president of Lincoln Center from 2002 to the present.

Crawford's tenure as chairman included a number of important accomplishments. Perhaps the most noteworthy was that by the end of 2004, all the Lincoln Center constituents had agreed in principle to the architects' plans for the 65th Street Redevelopment Project. The Metropolitan Opera had been particularly averse to the program at first, and Crawford's knowledge of and sensitivity to the Met's wishes played a major role in bringing it back into the fold. Maintaining the spirit of consensus and unanimity achieved under his watch will be crucial to the successful completion of the project.

The New York Philharmonic's dramatic, albeit brief, defection from the Lincoln Center family presented Crawford and Levy with another difficult crisis, which they managed with aplomb. When the orchestra subsequently abandoned its plans to leave Lincoln Center for Carnegie Hall, Philharmonic and Lincoln Center management agreed to work together in a more harmonious way to identify a mutually embraceable solution to the orchestra's complaints about Avery Fisher Hall.

While Crawford was chairman, Jazz at Lincoln Center, once a department of Lincoln Center and later spun off as its twelfth constituent, saw the completion of its new $131 million Frederick P. Rose Hall in the Time Warner Center, effectively extending the Center's geographic boundary several blocks southward. With Crawford's blessing, Lincoln Center played an important role in assisting Jazz in obtaining certain financial and legal arrangements that enabled its building program to proceed in the most efficient and effective way. Its new facilities, which opened with great fanfare in the fall of 2004, were met with critical and public acclaim.

In addition, Lincoln Center's programming efforts continued to expand and evolve under Crawford. Its long-running and much-beloved Mostly Mozart Festival, which had survived a four-day orchestra strike in 2002, was reinvigorated in a host of ways with the appointment of a new conductor, Louis Langrée, in December 2002. Another Center favorite, American Songbook, which premiered in 1999, expanded its offerings and relocated the majority of its presentations to the new Frederick P. Rose Hall.

Finally, Bruce Crawford was able, through the expansion of the Lincoln Center board of directors, to attract members who infused that body with new energy, varied perspectives, and valued expertise. By the time Crawford indicated to Lincoln Center insiders that he would leave his post as chairman in June 2005—Lincoln Center officially announced Crawford's intention to retire on January 13, 2005—the many pieces that would successfully launch the West 65th Street phase of the redevelopment program were in place.

Frank A. Bennack Jr., 2005–Present

Frank A. Bennack Jr., the former president and CEO of the Hearst Corporation, the communications giant, assumed the chairmanship of Lincoln Center's board of directors on June 20, 2005. As a member of the Lincoln Center board since 1994 and a vice chairman since 1999, as well as a managing director of the Metropolitan Opera Board, Mr. Bennack possessed the skills and the knowledge to make him a natural choice to succeed Bruce Crawford. "Frank's long experience and love of Lincoln Center, as well as his leadership at one of the largest and most successful media companies in the world, make him a superb choice for chairman," commented Crawford at the time of Bennack's election.[38]

The silver-haired Bennack is well known for being unflappable and for being a person who can evaluate important matters in an objective, efficient, and most pleasant manner. During the twenty-three years he headed Hearst, the company experienced a period of unprecedented growth and expansion. He began the process leading to the construction of the new Hearst Tower, designed by Sir Norman Foster, at 57th Street and Eighth Avenue. He now splits his time between Lincoln Center and the Hearst Corporation where he is vice chairman of the board and chairman of its executive committee.

Frank A. Bennack Jr., chairman of Lincoln Center from 2005 to the present.

Upon assuming the chairmanship of Lincoln Center, Bennack jumped in, working with Center president Reynold Levy on the pressing fundraising requirements of the Center's $459 million 65th Street Redevelopment Project. He recruited David M. Rubenstein, the managing director of the Carlyle Group, to serve as chairman of Bravo Lincoln Center, the capital campaign for the redevelopment project, and helped to recruit an outstanding group of individuals to serve on the campaign steering committee. "The fund-raising for redevelopment, and specifically for 65th Street, has gone even better than I would have expected," Bennack said after one year as chairman. "We have had a $200 million fund-raising year from private sources, which is arguably unprecedented. And, as I've gone around New York making these fund-raising calls with David Rubenstein and Reynold Levy, I've found an appreciation of Lincoln Center's importance as a civic and economic entity, along with its obvious greatness as a performing arts center. We've found a real interest in supporting that civic and economic role that I would not necessarily have expected. But I always did think that we could achieve what we were undertaking to achieve, that we could get redevelopment across the finish line and be proud of the outcome."[39]

In June 2006, Lincoln Center unveiled conceptual plans for the next phase of redevelopment, what the Center is calling the Promenade Project, which Bennack embraced. It will refurbish and reconfigure the Josie Robertson Plaza and the Columbus Avenue frontage, separating vehicular and pedestrian traffic and providing a gracious and welcoming entrance to the plaza. All constituents involved have approved the plans for the estimated $190 million improvement.

Bennack also set about expanding the Lincoln Center board. With a net increase of sixteen seats, the board now boasts an efficient mix of long-term members and a new generation, both in terms of age and people in leadership positions around the city who can help by lending expertise that the board might not otherwise have had access to. These changes were particularly useful, for example, when Lincoln Center issued its first tax-exempt bond issue, a complicated process made smoother by the board members' sound and informed advice. "The broader base of members, which is necessary when you are in the midst of such a massive undertaking, is critical," commented Reynold Levy. "I'm pleased to say that we've engaged them in a much broadened and energetic committee structure. Frank sets the tone, giving us an enormous amount of time and energy."[40]

Another area of interest to Bennack is finding ways to build on the "extraordinary cooperation we've gotten from the chairs and leadership of the constituent organizations in relation to the Center's redevelopment efforts."[41] For example, he initiated a new cross-campus marketing effort, asking the chairs of all the constituent organizations to appoint an influential member of the board to join a committee, chaired by Lincoln Center director Richard Braddock, to explore ways in which they can work together to better promote their various artistic offerings.

Further evidence of this spirit of collegiality can be seen in new collaborative efforts among the Lincoln Center family, producing the kind of programming excellence the Center's founders had envisioned. For example, the Lincoln Center Festival, in conjunction with the Metropolitan Opera, will present the Ring Cycle in July 2007, an enormous undertaking, and plans are under way for a collaboration between the Metropolitan Opera and the Lincoln Center Theater. "A lot of good things are going on at Lincoln Center," Bennack concluded. "I credit the foundation that was put in place during Beverly Sills and Bruce Crawford's tenures, and Reynold Levy's carrying forward what Nat Leventhal started. It's nice to be here at a time when those things are all in a more favorable, positive, and progressive state. I care about what goes on here."[42]

5

A NEW LOOK

Redevelopment and Renewal

BY THE END OF 1979, LINCOLN CENTER'S PUBLIC PLAZAS—the areas around the central fountain and the reflecting pool in front of the Vivian Beaumont Theater, and the small plaza in front of Alice Tully Hall—were in disrepair. Two decades of serious wear and tear—heavy pedestrian traffic, coupled with constant exposure to snow, sleet, sun, and rain—had left pavement slabs buckled, cracked, and worn. Walking there could be difficult and occasionally even dangerous. When it rained, there were leaks from the compromised areas into basement office spaces and the underground garage. Management knew it had to undertake significant repairs.

Because the City of New York owned the land on which Lincoln Center was built and thus was obligated to maintain the Center's outdoor areas, John Mazzola, the then Center president, turned for help in early 1980 to Henry Geldzahler, the commissioner of cultural affairs. The Koch administration at that time was dealing with a difficult economic climate and a tight budget but nonetheless found the $6 million needed to pay for the repairs. It insisted, however, that the Center's management supervise the project.

Later that same year, the architect Philip Johnson, working with a design team from Hurley & Farinella, completed plans for the restoration of Lincoln Center's public plazas and began to secure the necessary city approvals and obtain bids. The architects recommended that the original concrete surfaces be replaced with more durable granite, which had been used with great success in the construction of Damrosch Park in the 1960s.

Actual work on the plazas did not begin until mid-1982, the delay attributed to "difficulty in negotiating the contract with the city agencies."[1] The project was completed in the fall of 1982.

The 1990 opening of the Samuel B. and David Rose Building, the first addition to the Lincoln Center campus since its completion in 1969, helped bring into focus the increasingly pressing need to upgrade the physical plant. In addition, the New York Philharmonic and the New York City Opera, both troubled by inadequate facilities and difficult acoustics in their own halls, had commissioned preliminary studies of how to upgrade Avery Fisher Hall and the New York State Theater, respectively. Lincoln Center's resident organizations agreed that the Center needed to "undertake a major lead and coordinating role in helping to assess the capital needs throughout the campus and to spearhead an effort, which would also include efforts by the constituents themselves, to raise the funds necessary to realize the capital goals that might be developed."[2]

In response, chairman emeritus Martin E. Segal urged the board in 1998 to take a long-range look at several important issues facing Lincoln Center and its constituents.[3] The board established an ad hoc Committee for the 21st Century to study not only the condition of the physical plant but also the equally pressing issue of future audience development. This committee, headed by Vice Chairman of the Board Roy L. Furman, split into two subcommittees: one, under Alair Townsend, to consider redevelopment issues; the other, under Richard Braddock, audience development.

In April 1999, Lincoln Center engaged the architectural firm Beyer Blinder Bell (BBB), known for its sensitive redevelopment of landmark buildings, including New York City's Grand Central Terminal, to identify and assess all components of a Center-wide physical upgrade, make a set of recommendations that would address the campus's shortage of space, deteriorating facilities, and out-of-date technology, and suggest strategies for achieving the recommendations. Over an eight-month period, BBB worked intensively with each resident organization to determine its particular set of needs and wishes.

BBB published the results of its study, "Lincoln Center for the Performing Arts Capital Needs Survey," the first such survey ever undertaken at the Center. The document itemized what amounted to a constituents' "dream wish list." Estimated at $1.5 billion, the compendium of desired repairs, facility upgrades, and special projects represented a starting point for the enormous task at hand.[4] Center president Nathan Leventhal explained, "It will be the better part of a year before we have a sense of what is feasible to do and in what order it could be done."[5]

The $1.5 billion price tag proved newsworthy, although from the beginning Lincoln Center spokesmen insisted that not all wish-list items would or could be included in the final plan. The press also indulged in speculative opinion about the relative architectural

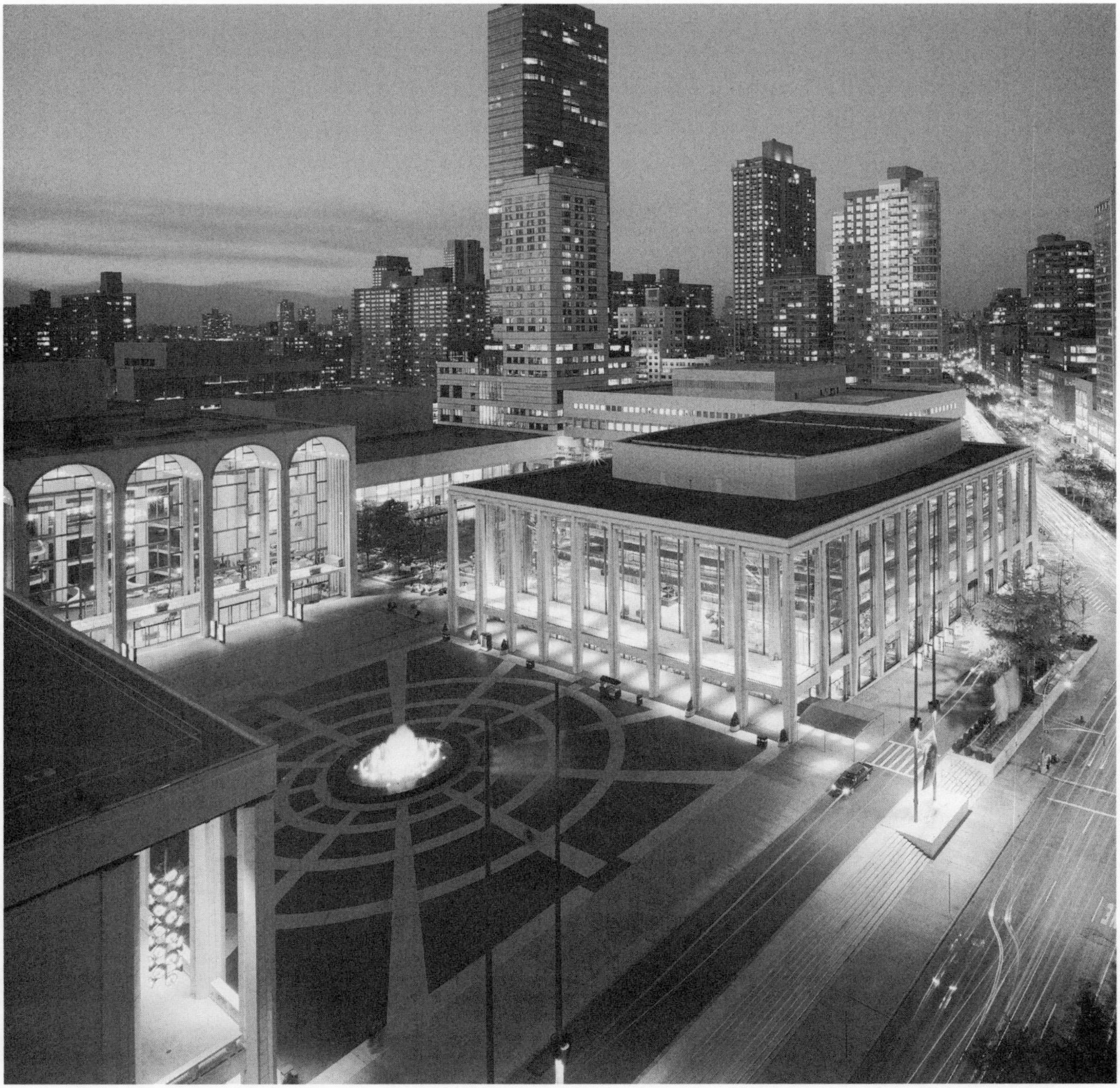

Aerial view of Lincoln Center and surrounding neighborhood at night.

merits and demerits of the Center's existing buildings, with some critics actually proffering the startling suggestion that the entire campus be blown up and rebuilt from the ground up.

At its December 1999 meeting, the board formally subscribed to a campus-wide renovation project and created a redevelopment committee, later to become known as the Lincoln Center Development Project, Inc. (LCDP). Its members included the chairs of all the Center resident organizations, plus the members of the Lincoln Center Council, all of whom were charged with carrying out the renovation project. The following summer, Rebecca Robertson, at that time the vice president for real estate at the Shubert Organization and formerly the president of the successful 42nd Street Redevelopment Project, was brought on as the staff person responsible for coordinating the creation of a redevelopment master plan. To begin the arduous process of detailing the possible components of a plan for Lincoln Center, Robertson worked with Beyer Blinder Belle; Cooper, Robertson & Partners; and Marshall Rose, LCDP's new chairman and a highly respected real-estate developer, who, as chairman of the New York Public Library, had overseen that institution's major renovation.

Before Nathan Leventhal retired as its president in December 2000, Lincoln Center negotiated an unprecedented funding agreement with the City of New York, whereby the city would contribute a total of $240 million toward redevelopment over the course of ten years at the rate of $24 million each year. Reportedly the largest sum ever given by the city to a cultural institution, it represented an important and encouraging element of the initial financial underpinnings of Lincoln Center's redevelopment program.

On January 1, 2001, Gordon J. Davis, a real-estate lawyer, a former city official in both the Lindsay and the Koch administrations, a longtime Lincoln Center board member, and the founding chairman of Jazz at Lincoln Center, took over as the seventh president of Lincoln Center. A significant portion of his work was to oversee plans for redevelopment of the Center's aging campus. On

January 18, Lincoln Center chairman Beverly Sills announced that the redevelopment effort had received an anonymous leadership gift of $15 million (later attributed to Michael R. Bloomberg, a Lincoln Center director for seven years prior to his election as mayor of New York City in November 2001).

Then, to the surprise of almost everyone, came the Metropolitan Opera Association's announcement that it was withdrawing from the project, "asserting it had not been given a proper role in planning the $1.5 billion redevelopment program."[6] Joseph Volpe, the general manager of the Met, and Paul M. Montrone, its president, stated that they had been "consistently excluded from meaningful participation in the process."[7] The Met was arguably the most powerful Lincoln Center constituent, and this seemed a troubling turn of events. According to speculation in the press, the heart of the defection was not what Volpe and Montrone had asserted, but rather their opposition to the plans to build a new home for the New York City Opera somewhere on the Lincoln Center campus, possibly in Damrosch Park. While Volpe and Montrone insisted that the real issues were the redevelopment project's "funding and the financial impact on the Met" and that their withdrawal "had nothing to do with the City Opera issue,"[8] these pronouncements did little to slow the swirl of speculation.

Yet the overriding belief on the part of Lincoln Center management and the eleven participating Lincoln Center organizations (Jazz at Lincoln Center and the New York Public Library for the Performing Arts, already in the thick of their own building projects, did not join the others) was that a campus overhaul was crucial to Lincoln Center's maintaining its position as the world's leading performing arts complex. Management's perseverance helped to stem the crisis, and, in May 2001, the Metropolitan Opera Association rejoined the project. The Met agreed to "remain on the board of the rebuilding effort at least until there is a vote on the master plan" and "receive thirty percent of the city money for rebuilding," whether or not it remained on the board.[9] Furthermore, all eleven participating organizations would have to agree to the master plan; if one dissented, the project would not proceed, and Lincoln Center would forfeit the city's first $24 million payment.

Over the spring and summer of 2001, Cooper, Robertson & Partners, along with the consultants Olin Partnership and Frank O. Gehry & Associates, worked up alternative plans for the Center's 6.3 acres of public spaces. Gehry's controversial idea to cover the entire fountain plaza area with a domelike glass structure was leaked prematurely to the press, where it received a less-than-enthusiastic reception. Many people at Lincoln Center reportedly opposed it as well, and the plan was dropped.

Rebecca Robertson, working with the participating constituents, further refined design alternatives for each hall and for the new facilities it was contemplating, and attached a preliminary price tag to each. Everyone involved hurried to complete the master plan, whose initial deadline was March 31, 2001, but was later postponed first to June 2001 and then to August 2001, before the plan finally was filed with the city in November of that year.

The impact of September 11, 2001, on Lincoln Center's redevelopment efforts cannot be underestimated. Suddenly, the prospects for raising what was soon revised downward to $1.2 billion seemed much less certain. A precipitous drop in box-office revenues, substantially reduced tourism, and anticipated cuts in city support prompted LCDP to take another look at the size and the scope of its projected redevelopment program. In response, Lincoln Center authorized a four-month study to determine (1) the appropriateness of the size and scale of the projects already considered; (2) the timing of the projects and possible revisions to the schedules already developed; (3) what incremental approach should be taken, if necessary, for the project; and (4) the feasibility of the participating constituents raising the money necessary in light of the changed economic environment.[10] Implicit in this agenda was the need to articulate and prioritize the real needs, rather than the dreams, of the participating institutions.

Amid a number of administrative difficulties, Gordon J. Davis resigned abruptly on September 27. Three weeks later, Marshall Rose also resigned, reportedly frustrated by the redevelopment project's slow progress and by major infighting among resident organizations.[11] In early January 2002, Janice Price, who had assumed Davis's duties as interim executive director of the Center, left Lincoln Center to head the new Kimmel Center in Philadelphia. Management seemed in disarray.

Then, in what represented a potential financial setback for redevelopment, Michael R. Bloomberg, shortly after he took office as mayor on January 1, 2002, announced that "construction projects such as the planned Lincoln Center refurbishments probably would be put on hold while the city recovers from the impact of the World Trade Center attacks and the weakened economy."[12] The next month, the city said that while it would make good on its initial $24 million payment to Lincoln Center, it would stretch out the remainder of the committed $240 million, "deferring payment of some of the remaining money to the out years."[13]

Into this difficult situation stepped Martin J. Oppenheimer, the chairman of the board of the City Center of Music and Drama, who agreed to become interim head of LCDP, assuming Marshall Rose's responsibilities. Among the pressing challenges he faced were securing promised city funding in a new and difficult economic environment and resolving the outstanding planning issues surrounding the campus's public areas.

On May 1, 2002, Reynold Levy, the president of the International Rescue Committee, became president of Lincoln Center. It was a particularly difficult time in the Center's history. New York City's economy, weakened in the aftermath of September 11, had made fund-raising for redevelopment ever more challenging. In June, Levy was joined by Bruce Crawford, the former president and general manager of the Metropolitan Opera and the chairman of Omnicom Group, as chairman of Lincoln Center.

By July, the team of Crawford and Levy, citing the changed economic environment, told the press that Lincoln Center needed to reassess the project's scope and cost. "What we would like to do and what can be realistically done: We need to address that issue, and we will," Crawford told the *New York Times*.[14] He also acknowledged two major problems confronting Lincoln Center's redevelopment efforts: the problematic acoustics in both Avery Fisher Hall and the New York State Theater and the potential move off-campus of the New York City Opera.

Gradually, though, plans for redevelopment evolved, and a more modest approach to all aspects of the project emerged. Rebuilding would be completed in phases over a ten-year period, thus minimizing disruption to ongoing performance schedules in each of the halls under renovation. LCDP formed working groups to help devise plans for the Center's four primary public spaces—West 65th Street, the North Plaza, the Josie Robertson Plaza, and Damrosch Park.

With the pro bono assistance of McKinsey & Company and its senior partner David Hunt, Lincoln Center established a capital campaign to support the projected ten-year redevelopment program.[15] Rosemarie Garipoli, the former principal fund-raiser for the New York Botanical Garden and the Solomon R. Guggenheim Foundation, was brought on as executive director of the campaign, which would become known as Bravo Lincoln Center.

Peter Lehrer, the cofounder of Lehrer McGovern Bovis, was named the new chairman of LCDP, succeeding Martin Oppenheimer. A search committee invited five architects to submit plans for the 6.3 acres of open space. Eventually, they selected the cutting-edge firm Diller Scofidio + Renfro, which would work in association with Fox & Fowle Architects; Cooper, Robertson & Partners as planners; L'Observatoire as lighting designers; Olin Partnership as landscape architects; and 2 × 4 as graphic designers.

The team's first order of business was to "transform 65th Street between Broadway and Amsterdam into Lincoln Center's 'Main Street,' making it more pedestrian-friendly, opening up the campus to the surrounding community, and creating lively new street-level entrances and an identity for Lincoln Center's seven constituents and twelve performance venues that front the road."[16] The resident organizations to be affected by this phase of redevelopment were the Juilliard School, the Chamber Music Society of Lincoln Center, the Film Society of Lincoln Center, the School of American Ballet, the Lincoln Center Theater, the New York Public Library for the Performing Arts, and Lincoln Center for the Performing Arts, Inc.

It appeared momentarily that Crawford and Levy had smoothed troubled waters and that plans were on track for a successful, if somewhat scaled-back, redevelopment effort. "This is not what we would like to have; it is what is necessary," Center chairman Bruce Crawford told the *New York Times* in May. "These are not luxuries. . . . Lincoln Center's theaters and public spaces have to be improved and maintained. You can't go decades without bringing them up-to-date."[17]

Then, however, in June 2003, Peter Lehrer resigned, telling the press that the Center's redevelopment project was "wasteful and badly managed" and publicly (but unsuccessfully) calling for Rebecca Robertson's resignation.[18] Ten days earlier, Lincoln Center officials, working with the New York Philharmonic to explore alternatives for an eventual renovation of Avery Fisher Hall, had been broadsided by the Philharmonic's surprise announcement that it had agreed in principle to move to and merge with Carnegie Hall. The Philharmonic fracas resolved itself four months later, however, when the orchestra announced that it had abandoned the move. Yet the potential impact on future redevelopment efforts of these two very public instances of discord was unsettling.

In the spring of 2004, Lincoln Center unveiled Diller Scofidio + Renfro's innovative conceptual plans for the redesign of West 65th Street and the North Plaza. The architects' design united West 65th Street with the surrounding cityscape, extending the threshold of Lincoln Center and opening up the campus to

encourage the interaction of artists, students, and the public. It appeared to embrace the spirit of the original 1960s architecture, while incorporating elements of transparency and fluidity to create a new language celebrating the vitality of the cultural complex today.[19] In addition to benefits to be enjoyed by all constituents, such as improved street access, enhanced public spaces, the 65th Street Redevelopment Project included benefits specific to each participating constituent. They were

View of North Plaza across the redesigned reflecting pool, with new lawn over the restaurant, as designed by Diller Scofidio + Renfro.

Juilliard Expansion and new Alice Tully Hall lobby, as designed by Diller Scofidio + Renfro.

- *The Juilliard School*: a new music technology center; an orchestra rehearsal room; a black-box theater; a dance studio; practice rooms and classrooms to accommodate its new jazz program; and a street-level box office.
- *The Film Society*: two new screening rooms; an amphitheater-style public space for lectures, symposia, and educational offerings; and a highly visible street presence to enhance walk-up sales.

- *Lincoln Center Theater*: a new black-box theater; a reception area; an expanded street-level public lobby; and a dramatic new West 65th Street entrance.
- *The Chamber Music Society*: the benefits of a complete modernization and expansion of Alice Tully Hall.
- *Lincoln Center, Inc.*: improvements to the Samuel B. and David Rose Building, including a glass-enclosed lobby providing increased security, a new pedestrian circulation hub, and a strong street presence for all the Rose Building's tenants and facilities; the renovation of Alice Tully Hall, in which much of Lincoln Center's own programming is presented; and redesigned outdoor public spaces.

Interior view of Alice Tully Hall, as designed by Diller Scofidio + Renfro.

The architects' schematics were heralded both in the Center's boardroom and in the press. The *New York Times*'s architecture critic, Herbert Muschamp, wrote, "Lincoln Center Redevelopment Project has found itself a fine, mellow groove. What we've got here is the inverse of the Wow Factor: a new plan for the Center's public spaces so understated as to seem almost uncanny. It looks just like Lincoln Center, only smarter, more self-aware and amazingly confident in its sense of direction."[20] Justin Davidson of *Newsday* added that the prospect of "stripping away walls and architectural barnacles and replacing them with glass" was exciting. "Rather than hunkering behind battlements of travertine, the theaters, schools and performance institutions along 65th Street will let entertainment spill into the street."[21]

Every Lincoln Center constituent was required to, and eventually did, approve Diller Scofidio + Renfro's preliminary plans for West 65th Street and the campus's North Plaza area, which management referred to as the "second" phase of its redevelopment (the first phase consisting of planning and early infrastructure improvements, paid for with the city's first $24 million). The board singled out Bruce Kovner, the Lincoln Center director and chairman of the 65th Street Working Group, for special credit in achieving this rare and welcome show of solidarity and support.

After having initially approved the preliminary plans, however, it appeared that the Metropolitan Opera might delay the project with its insistence that it have direct access to the West 65th Street garage, something Diller Scofidio + Renfro's plans did not include. Eventually, a solution was devised and the Met was mollified.

As 2004 drew to a close, three significant developments were worth noting. First, Lincoln Center's plans for West 65th Street were submitted to the City Planning Commission, thus initiating the seven-month Uniform Land Use Review Procedure (ULURP) process during which necessary governmental approvals (as well as enthusiastic community board approval) were obtained. The ULURP process, according to Reynold Levy, went extremely smoothly, a notable achievement for a project located on the West Side of Manhattan, where unanimity is rarely the order of the day among often contentious neighborhood groups.[22] Second, the South Campus Working Group, headed by the New York City Ballet board member and New York builder Daniel Brodsky, and including representatives from the City Center for Music and Drama, the New York City Opera, the New York City Ballet, the New York Philharmonic, and the Metropolitan Opera, began to look at possible changes to Josie Robertson Plaza, Damrosch Park, and the West 62nd Street perimeter. Finally, Lincoln Center and the New York Philharmonic achieved significant progress in their consideration of the particulars of a future Avery Fisher Hall renovation, slated to begin after the scheduled completion in 2009 of the 65th Street Redevelopment Project.

Design work was under way on two additional phases of redevelopment—the South Campus and Avery Fisher Hall. The South Campus Working Group eventually articulated eleven recommendations for the public spaces within its area, which were shared with the architects Diller Scofidio + Renfro. Still at issue, however, was whether the New York City Opera would (1) leave the Lincoln Center campus altogether; (2) acquire, and subsequently build on, the Red Cross Building site on the northwest corner of West 65th Street and Amsterdam Avenue, thereby extending Lincoln Center's geographic boundaries immediately northward and westward; or (3) remain in a renovated and improved New York State Theater.

And, second, the New York Philharmonic and Lincoln Center together retained the internationally acclaimed architect Sir Norman Foster to draw up initial plans for a renovation of Avery Fisher Hall, based largely on the successful June 2004 experiment that extended forward the Avery Fisher Hall stage. Foster submitted these plans to Lincoln Center and the New York Philharmonic in early 2005. The Executive Committee of the Lincoln Center board then authorized a detailed feasibility study of these recommendations.[23]

At its March 2005 meeting, the Lincoln Center board, having obtained authorization by the boards of the participating resident organizations, voted to proceed with the 65th Street Redevelopment Project.[24] Lead gift fund-raising was well under way, and a "prudent, credible plan" in place for raising the balance.[25]

Once Lincoln Center had the unanimous approval of the resident organizations to be affected by the program, work on the 65th Street Redevelopment Project proceeded at a lively pace. In June 2005, newly elected chairman Frank A. Bennack Jr. asked David M. Rubenstein, the vice chair of Lincoln Center's board and the managing director of the Carlyle Group, to head the Center's $459 million fund-raising campaign, Bravo Lincoln Center. Rubenstein enthusiastically accepted. "I am honored to serve as Campaign Chair, and look forward to working with Lincoln Center's committed board and talented professional staff," he said.[26] With the effective assistance of the campaign Steering Committee—Frank A. Bennack Jr., Barbara H. Block, Richard S. Braddock, Richard K. DeScherer, Blair W. Effron, Joel S. Ehrenkranz, Katherine Farley, Roy L. Furman, Rita E. Hauser, Bruce Kovner, Reynold Levy, Peter L. Malkin, Indra Nooyi, and Thomas A. Renyi—working with Rosemarie Garopoli, the campaign's executive director, Bravo Lincoln Center had, by June 2006, already raised 75 percent of Lincoln Center's share of the project's costs.

In March 2006, Diller Scofidio + Renfro's final plans for selected elements of the 65th Street Redevelopment Project were formally approved, as well as the architects' conceptual plans for a pedestrian bridge over West 65th Street. That same month, Katherine Farley was named chairman of the Lincoln Center Development Project, and Jerry Hastings, the senior vice president of Lincoln Center, took on the added responsibility of executive director of the Development Project, replacing Rebecca Robertson, who left to become president and CEO of a new visual and performing-arts organization to be housed in the Seventh Regiment Armory.

Ground breaking for Lincoln Center's ten-year redevelopment program took place on June 12, 2006, with Mayor Michael R. Bloomberg in attendance. The actual demolition and construction

on the West 65th Street portion—the first to be undertaken—will commence during the summer of 2006. Completion of the entire project is scheduled for the end of 2009, Lincoln Center's fiftieth anniversary.

Ground-breaking ceremony, Lincoln Center Redevelopment Project, June 12, 2006. Pictured, from left: Liz Diller, Reynold Levy, Katherine Farley, Mayor Michael R. Bloomberg, Frank A. Bennack Jr., and David Rubenstein.

On the same day, Lincoln Center unveiled Diller Scofidio + Renfro's plans for upgrading the Josie Robertson Plaza and the campus's Columbus Avenue frontage, creating a new entrance to the Center devoid of vehicular drop-off traffic, which will be rerouted below grade. Lincoln Center's board agreed to raise up to an additional $45 million for "the renovation for the Columbus Avenue frontage, Josie Robertson Plaza, certain facility graphics, and a portion of the Central Mechanical Plant."

In another initiative, Lincoln Center also announced in June 2006 that it had reached an agreement in principle to lease the underutilized, privately owned, seven-thousand-square-foot

New grand stair and Josie Robertson Plaza, as designed by Diller Scofidio + Renfro.

Harmony Atrium, located between Broadway and Columbus Avenue and between West 62nd and West 63rd Streets. Lincoln Center hopes to turn it into a lively gathering place and a central information center for tourists and students. Visitors will be able to obtain discounted tickets to Center events on a "day of" basis. In addition, it will be used for community groups.

Of the estimated $650 million price tag for the 65th Street Redevelopment Project, Lincoln Center's share will total $459 million. Funds will come from private sources such as corporations, foundations, and individual givers, as well as the federal, state, and city governments. New York City's anticipated contribution to the West 65th Street work would be somewhere between $60 million and $90 million. Of Lincoln Center's $459 million share, $51 million will go directly to the West 65th Street constituents to help with their redevelopment expenses. This is one of the unique and most compelling aspects of the 65th Street Redevelopment Project: the assumption by Lincoln Center, Inc., of a generous portion of each participating resident organization's fund-raising burden.

"We've taken on a significant set of financial responsibilities," said Center president Reynold Levy. "We've agreed to coordinate and pay for all planning costs associated with redevelopment. We've agreed to administer and pay for the single consolidated fund-raising effort. We've agreed to assume full financial responsibility for the changes to the outdoor public areas and to the changes to the Rose Building that all its tenants will enjoy. We've agreed to match a portion of the funds the constituents raise, which is unprecedented in Lincoln Center's history."[27]

The strong leadership Lincoln Center exerted in all these efforts contributed greatly to the sense of unanimity and the climate of cooperation that were necessary to moving ahead. "I think among any federation of a dozen constituencies, the concept of unanimity is indeed difficult to attain," commented former Center chairman Bruce Crawford. "There are always conflicting objectives at times. It's been difficult. But I think that basically we got to a point where it became apparent that there was a greater good here. And Lincoln Center took a much more aggressive role in sorting these things out and in assuming strong leadership. There was quite a bit of care given to not doing things that would be harmful to a constituent."[28]

To have come this far in its redevelopment effort is an outstanding achievement on the part of Lincoln Center and its constituents. Having struggled through a number of challenging difficulties and seemingly inevitable setbacks, Lincoln Center is now poised to begin the next phase of its formidable undertaking—making real in the twenty-first century what has for years been only a dream for this fifty-year-old performing arts complex: a revitalized, vibrant, exciting, and beautiful campus—a cultural oasis where artists, students, patrons, and visitors from around the world will continue to find something that will transport, inspire, and transform them. "There's a wonderful spirit here of energy and purposefulness," said Reynold Levy. "I really do believe that those who planned Lincoln Center would be happy to see what's being created now. There are a lot of people around who believe Lincoln Center is worth reinvesting in now, in a major way, for the next generation of audiences."[29]

CHRONOLOGY 1955–2006

APRIL 1955	Robert Moses initiates the Lincoln Square Urban Renewal Project.
DECEMBER 1955	The Exploratory Committee meets to discuss creating a musical arts center.
JUNE 1956	Lincoln Center for the Performing Arts, Inc., is incorporated; John D. Rockefeller 3rd is elected president of Lincoln Center.
NOVEMBER 1956	The New York Philharmonic becomes a constituent; its area of primacy is symphonic music.
FEBRUARY 1957	The Juilliard School becomes a constituent; its area of primacy is professional education in the performing arts.
	The Metropolitan Opera Association becomes a constituent; its area of primacy is opera and classical operetta.

FEBRUARY 1958	Lincoln Center purchases the land from West 62nd to West 65th Streets, and from Columbus Avenue to Amsterdam Avenue, from the City of New York for $3.9 million.
JULY 1958	Demolition of existing buildings on the site begins; it is completed by May 1960.
MAY 1959	Lincoln Center for the Performing Arts, Inc., breaks ground, with President Dwight D. Eisenhower in attendance.
FEBRUARY 1960	The Repertory Theater Association becomes a constituent; its area of primacy is drama.
JUNE 1960	The Lincoln Center Youth Program (aka Lincoln Center Student Program) is established.
JANUARY 1961	John D. Rockefeller 3rd relinquishes the presidency of Lincoln Center to become its first chairman.
	General Maxwell D. Taylor is elected president of Lincoln Center but resigns six months later when recalled to active duty.
JANUARY 1962	William Schuman assumes the presidency of Lincoln Center.
AUGUST 1962	The List Poster and Print Program is inaugurated with the release of the Ben Shahn work commemorating the opening of Philharmonic Hall.
SEPTEMBER 1962	Philharmonic Hall (later named Avery Fisher Hall) opens, the first Lincoln Center hall to do so.
OCTOBER 1962	The New York Music Theater, Inc. (later known as the Music Theater of Lincoln Center, Inc.), becomes a constituent; its area of primacy is operetta and musical comedy.

AUGUST 1963	August Fanfare, Lincoln Center's first summer program, debuts.
SEPTEMBER 1963	The New York Film Festival opens in Philharmonic Hall.
APRIL 1964	The New York State Theater opens.
	The fountain on the plaza begins operating.
APRIL 1965	The Education Department, the forerunner of the Lincoln Center Institute, is created.
	The City Center of Music and Drama, Inc., becomes a constituent; its area of primacy is the ballet.
SEPTEMBER 1965	Henry Moore's sculpture *Reclining Figure* is installed in the North Plaza reflecting pool.
OCTOBER 1965	The Vivian Beaumont Theater and the Forum (now named the Mitzi Newhouse Theater) open.
	The Great Performers series opens.
NOVEMBER 1965	The New York Public Library becomes a constituent; its area of primacy is the circulation and study of printed materials and musical recordings and the operation of a specialized museum of the performing arts.
	The Library and Museum of the Performing Arts opens.
JANUARY 1966	The New York City Board of Estimate approves the future sale of the High School of Commerce (later to become known as the Brandeis High School Annex) to Lincoln Center.
AUGUST 1966	Midsummer Serenades: A Mozart Festival (now known as the Mostly Mozart Festival) begins.

SEPTEMBER 1966	The Metropolitan Opera House is inaugurated.
JUNE 1967	Lincoln Center Festival '67 opens.
JUNE 1968	John Mazzola is appointed chief executive officer of Lincoln Center; he becomes managing director in 1970 and president in May 1977; he resigns in 1982.
MAY 1969	Damrosch Park and the Guggenheim Bandshell open.
SEPTEMBER 1969	Alice Tully Hall opens.
OCTOBER 1969	The Juilliard School building opens, completing the original campus.
MARCH 1970	The Music Theater of Lincoln Center, Inc., becomes an inactive constituent.
MAY 1970	Amyas Ames is elected chairman of the board; he serves until June 1, 1981.
	The Consolidated Corporate Fund Drive is established.
AUGUST 1971	The Everyman-Community Street Theater Festival is launched.
NOVEMBER 1971	Great Performers introduces a series devoted to folk, rock, and jazz.
DECEMBER 1971	The first holiday tree is lit at Lincoln Center; the Community Holiday Festival debuts (the annual event runs until 1993).
MAY 1972	The Chamber Music Society of Lincoln Center becomes a constituent.
JULY 1972	Mostly Mozart is given its official name.

MAY 1973	The New York Shakespeare Festival becomes a theater constituent.
JUNE 1973	The Repertory Theater of Lincoln Center ceases to be a constituent as of its last performance.
SEPTEMBER 1973	Philharmonic Hall is renamed Avery Fisher Hall.
MAY 1974	The Lincoln Center Institute for the Arts in Education is founded.
AUGUST 1974	The Lincoln Center Out of Doors summer festival is launched.
SEPTEMBER 1974	The Music Theater of Lincoln Center, Inc., ceases to be a constituent.
OCTOBER 1974	The Avery Fisher Artist Program is established, including the Avery Fisher Prize and the Avery Fisher Career Grants; the Great Performers series is devoted to jazz.
NOVEMBER 1974	The Film Society of Lincoln Center, which was organized in 1969, becomes a constituent.
1975	The Meet-the-Artist program is created.
JANUARY 1976	The first telecast of *Live from Lincoln Center* airs.
MAY 1976	The Directors Emeriti Council is established.
OCTOBER 1976	Avery Fisher Hall reopens after an acoustical renovation.
AUGUST 1977	The New York Shakespeare Festival ceases to be a constituent.
MAY 1979	The twentieth anniversary of the ground breaking is celebrated.

JULY 1980	The Vivian Beaumont Theater, Inc., becomes a constituent; in October, it changes its name to Lincoln Center Theater.
JUNE 1981	Martin E. Segal is elected chairman of the board; he serves until June 1986.
DECEMBER 1981	The Chairman's Council category of donors is added to the Associates of Lincoln Center fund-raising program.
SEPTEMBER 1982	The New York State Theater reopens after an acoustical reconstruction.
MARCH 1983	Glenn W. Ferguson is named president of Lincoln Center; he serves until January 1984.
JUNE 1984	Nathan Leventhal is elected president of Lincoln Center; he retires in December 2000.
JANUARY 1985	The Committee on the Future of Lincoln Center is established; it issues a report in May 1986.
JUNE 1986	George Weissman is elected chairman of the board; he serves until June 1994.
	The Martin E. Segal Award for Young Performers is established.
SEPTEMBER 1986	The board votes to acquire the site of the former Brandeis High School to begin a new building project.
MAY 1987	The School of American Ballet becomes a constituent.
JULY 1987	Serious Fun! is created.
AUGUST 1987	Classical Jazz begins.

NOVEMBER 1987	Ground breaking begins for a new building, soon to be known as the Samuel B. and David Rose Building.
JULY 1989	Midsummer Night Swing begins.
JUNE 1990	The Department of Jazz is created.
NOVEMBER 1990	The Samuel B. and David Rose Building opens.
DECEMBER 1990	A major grant from the Fan Fox and Leslie R. Samuels Foundation is given to launch the commissioning fund.
JANUARY 1991	The Mozart Bicentennial opens; it lasts through August 1992.
MAY 1991	A $3.2 million grant from the Lila Wallace–Reader's Digest Fund is awarded to the Lincoln Center Institute for the Arts in Education.
DECEMBER 1991	The Walter Reade Theater opens.
SEPTEMBER 1992	Avery Fisher Hall reopens after acoustical modifications.
JANUARY 1993	Lincoln Center Institute for the Arts in Education creates the Association of Institutes for Aesthetic Education.
JANUARY 1994	*Backstage\Lincoln Center* is inaugurated.
JUNE 1994	Beverly Sills is elected chairman of the board; she retires in May 2002.
AUGUST 1994	The Lincoln Center Community Arts Projects begins; it ends in 1999.
FEBRUARY 1996	*Live from Lincoln Center* celebrates its twenty-fifth anniversary.

JULY 1996	Jazz at Lincoln Center (the former Department of Jazz) becomes a full constituent; Lincoln Center Festival '96 launches a summer festival program.
NOVEMBER 1996	The Reel to Real children's series begins as a joint collaboration between Lincoln Center, Inc., and the Film Society of Lincoln Center.
JULY 1997	The Paul Milstein Plaza is dedicated.
SEPTEMBER 1998	The fountain plaza is renamed for Josie Robertson.
NOVEMBER 1998	The Committee for the 21st Century convenes its first meeting.
JANUARY 1999	The New Visions series, part of Great Performers, begins.
FEBRUARY 1999	The American Songbook series is launched.
MAY 1999	*TimeSculpture*, designed by Philip Johnson, is installed in Dante Park opposite Lincoln Center.
JULY 2000	Mostly Mozart opens the season with its first free outdoor concert.
OCTOBER 2000	Great Performers inaugurates its The Spoken Word series.
JANUARY 2001	Gordon J. Davis is elected president of Lincoln Center (he resigns on September 27, 2001); Lincoln Center Development Project, Inc., is established to manage redevelopment of Lincoln Center.
SEPTEMBER 2001	Juilliard creates the Juilliard Institute for Jazz Studies in conjunction with Jazz at Lincoln Center.
MAY 2002	Reynold Levy becomes president of Lincoln Center.

AUGUST 2002	Bruce Crawford is elected chairman of Lincoln Center for the Performing Arts, Inc.; he retires in June 2005.
FEBRUARY 2003	Diller Scofidio + Renfro is selected to redesign Lincoln Center's public spaces.
DECEMBER 2003	Prints from the List Print and Poster Collection are exhibited at Art Basel/Miami, the premier contemporary art show in North America.
APRIL 2004	Plans for the West 65th Street portion of Lincoln Center's redevelopment are unveiled to critical acclaim; Bravo Lincoln Center, redevelopment's capital campaign, is officially launched.
NOVEMBER 2004	The Consolidated Corporate Fund changes its name to the Lincoln Center Corporate Fund.
	Jazz at Lincoln Center opens its new $128 million Frederick P. Rose Hall facilities in the Time Warner Center.
JUNE 2005	Frank A. Bennack Jr. is named chairman of Lincoln Center; David M. Rubenstein, the vice chairman of Lincoln Center, is named chairman of the redevelopment's capital campaign.
JANUARY 2006	Lincoln Center, Inc., issues its first tax-exempt municipal bonds to help support redevelopment.
FEBRUARY 2006	The Lincoln Center Institute celebrates its thirtieth anniversary.
MARCH 2006	The Lincoln Center Development Project Board unanimously approves final plans for selected elements of the 65th Street Redevelopment Project; conceptual plans for the West 65th Street

pedestrian bridge and for the Josie Robertson Plaza and the Columbus Avenue frontage are also approved.

MAY 2006 — *Live from Lincoln Center* celebrates its thirtieth on-air anniversary.

JUNE 2006 — Official ground breaking is held for the 65th Street Redevelopment Project; Bravo Lincoln Center launches the public phase of its capital campaign; Lincoln Center announces an agreement in principle with the owner of Harmony Atrium to revitalize this underused, privately owned space into a new interdisciplinary public venue.

(Adapted from "Chronology: Lincoln Center History," courtesy of Judith Johnson, archivist, Lincoln Center for the Performing Arts, Inc.)

LINCOLN CENTER FOR THE PERFORMING ARTS, INC.

Board of Directors
As of June 26, 2006

Frank A. Bennack Jr. (1994), Chairman
Katherine G. Farley (2003), Vice Chairman
Roy L. Furman (1989), Vice Chairman
Bruce Kovner (2001), Vice Chairman
David M. Rubenstein (2004), Vice Chairman
Ann Ziff (1995), Vice Chairman
Harvey Golub (1999), Treasurer
Susan Rudin (2003), Chair, Lincoln Center Institute

Robert J. Alexander (2004)
Susan L. Baker (2004)
John B. Beinecke (2005)
Renee E. Belfer (1996)
Albert C. Bellas (1988)
Mrs. Barbara H. Block (1994)

Richard S. Braddock (1990)
Susan S. Braddock (2005)
Diane M. Coffey (1992)
Zoe Cruz (2006)
Lewis Cullman (2005)
Richard K. DeScherer (2003)
Dinyar Devitre (2002)
Blair W. Effron (2003)
Joel S. Ehrenkranz (2003)
Richard L. Fisher (1996)
Peter Frelinghuysen (2005)
Barry S. Friedberg (2003)
Bart Friedman (2002)
Stephanie George (2005)
Efraim Grinberg (2001)
Mrs. Audrey Gruss (1989)
Paul B. Guenther (1996)
William B. Harrison Jr. (2006)
Gurnee F. Hart (2004)
Rita E. Hauser (1996)
David A. Hunt (2002)
Carl C. Icahn (2004)
Robert A. Iger (1995)
Ros L'Esperance (2006)
Thomas H. Lee (1995)
Nathan Leventhal (2001)
Reynold Levy (2002)
Dr. Frayda B. Lindemann (1999)
Peter L. Malkin, Esq. (1979)
Sir Deryck Maughan (2002)
Raymond J. McGuire (2005)
Philip L. Milstein (2005)
William C. Morris (2003)
Indra K. Nooyi (2003)
Martin J. Oppenheimer, Esq. (1984)
Hideaki Otaka (2004)
Joseph R. Perella (2000)
Thomas A. Renyi (2000)
Julian H. Robertson Jr. (1998)
Stephen M. Ross (2006)
Lisa Schiff (2002)
Stefan M. Selig (2005)
Jeffrey B. Soref (2003)
Mrs. Paul (Daisy) Soros (1992)
Julien J. Studley (1993)
Laurie M. Tisch (2004)
Doreen A. Toben (2004)
Alair A. Townsend (1993)
Christopher J. Williams (2004)
John Wren (2005)
Motokazu Yoshida (2005)

Ex Officio

Hon. Michael R. Bloomberg (2002), Mayor, the City of New York

Hon. Patricia E. Harris (Mayoral Designee), Deputy Mayor for Administration

Hon. Christine C. Quinn (2006), Speaker of the New York City Council

Hon. Marcel Van Ooyen (Speaker's Designate), Deputy Chief of Staff

Hon. Kate D. Levin (2002), Commissioner, Department of Cultural Affairs

Hon. Adrian Benepe (2002), Commissioner, Department of Parks and Recreation

Directors Emeriti

Willard C. Butcher
Bruce Crawford
Louis V. Gerstner Jr.
Victor Gotbaum
Eugene P. Grisanti
Mary Rodgers Guettel
Mrs. Leon Hess
Ruth W. Houghton
Mrs. Gilbert W. Humphrey
H. Frederick Krimendahl II
June Noble Larkin
Hon. Anthony D. Marshall
William F. May
Sandra Priest Rose
Irwin Schneiderman
Martin E. Segal, Chairman Emeritus
Walter V. Shipley
Beverly Sills
Howard Solomon
Carl Spielvogel
Stephen Stamas
Dr. Frank Stanton
Ronald P. Stanton
Lillian Vernon
George Weissman, Chairman Emeritus
Edgar B. Young
Mrs. Whitney M. Young Jr.

Senior Staff

As of June 26, 2006

PRESIDENT	Reynold Levy
SENIOR VICE PRESIDENT	Gerald A. Hastings
VICE PRESIDENTS	Nan Keeton, Marketing & Business Development
	Jane S. Moss, Programming
	Liza Parker, Human Resources & Administrative Services
	Tamar C. Podell, Planning and Development
	Lesley Friedman Rosenthal, General Counsel & Secretary
	Seema Reedy, Consumer Ventures
	Daniel Rubin, Finance
	Betsy Vorce, Public Relations
EXECUTIVE DIRECTOR, CAPITAL CAMPAIGN	Rosemarie Garipoli
EXECUTIVE PRODUCER, TELEVISION	John Goberman
EXECUTIVE DIRECTOR, LINCOLN CENTER INSTITUTE	Scott Noppe-Brandon
DIRECTOR, LINCOLN CENTER FESTIVAL	Nigel Redden

Lincoln Center Council

As of June 26, 2006

The Chamber Music Society of Lincoln Center, Inc.
Norma Hurlburt, Executive Director

The City Center of Music and Drama
Martin J. Oppenheimer, Chairman

The Film Society of Lincoln Center, Inc.
Claudia Bonn, Executive Vice President

Jazz at Lincoln Center
Kathy Brown, Executive Director

The Juilliard School
Joseph W. Polisi, President

Lincoln Center Institute
Scott Noppe-Brandon, Executive Director

Lincoln Center for the Performing Arts, Inc.
Reynold Levy, President

The Lincoln Center Theater
Bernard Gersten, Executive Producer

The Metropolitan Opera Association, Inc.
Peter Gelb, General Manager

The New York City Ballet
Peter Martins, Ballet Master in Chief

The New York City Opera
Paul Kellogg, General & Artistic Director

The New York Public Library for the Performing Arts, Inc.
Jacqueline Z. Davis, Executive Director

The Philharmonic-Symphony Society of New York, Inc.
Zarin Mehta, President & Executive Director

The School of American Ballet, Inc.
Marjorie Van Dercook, Executive Director

NOTES

The source for Lincoln Center Executive Committee Minutes, Lincoln Center Board of Directors Minutes, and Oral Histories is the Lincoln Center for the Performing Arts, Inc., Archives. The Oral Histories are a collection of taped and transcribed interviews conducted by Sharon Zane from 1990 to 2001.

The abbreviation LCPA indicates the Lincoln Center for the Performing Arts, Inc., Archives.

Introduction

1. John D. Rockefeller 3rd, speech on the occasion of his retirement from Lincoln Center, June 23, 1970, Edgar B. Young, *Lincoln Center: The Building of an Institution* (New York: New York University Press, 1980), p. 304.
2. John D. Rockefeller 3rd, address, delivered on the occasion of receiving the Gold Baton Award, American Symphony Orchestra League, San Francisco, Ca., June 22, 1963, LCPA.
3. "Lincoln Center's Big Bash," *Time*, June 4, 1979.
4. Paul Goldberger, "Architecture: Lincoln Center and Changes Wrought by 20 Years," *New York Times*, May 21, 1979.
5. Richard Shepard, "Lincoln Center—The First 20 Years," *New York Times*, May 20, 1979.

6. Ibid.
7. Message from President Jimmy Carter to Lincoln Center on the occasion of its twentieth anniversary, May 1979.
8. Irving Kolodin, "Lincoln Center at 20: Old," *Newsday*, May 13, 1979.
9. Richard Shepard, "Lincoln Center—The First 20 Years," *New York Times*, May 20, 1979.
10. Ibid.
11. "Report on Survey to Determine the Feasibility of Creating and Operating a Performing Arts Center in New York City," Day & Zimmerman, Engineers, 1955, LCPA.

Chapter 1. All in the Family: Lincoln Center and Its Constituents

1. Lincoln Center Executive Committee Minutes, September 20, 1962.
2. Lincoln Center Executive Committee Minutes, October 25, 1962.
3. William Schuman Oral History, 1990.
4. Herbert Kupferberg, *New York Herald Tribune*, July 7, 1964.
5. Henry Guettel Oral History, 1992.
6. Ibid.
7. Sam Zolotow, "Rodgers Theater Battles Deficits," *New York Times*, February 16, 1966.
8. Ibid.
9. Lincoln Center Executive Committee Minutes, October 3, 1967.
10. Jack Gaver, "Musical Blackout," *Cincinnati Post*, July 3, 1970.
11. Lincoln Center Executive Committee Minutes, September 24, 1974.
12. William Schuman Oral History, 1990.
13. Amos Vogel Oral History, 1993.
14. Martin E. Segal Oral History, 1991.
15. William Schuman Oral History, 1990.
16. Martin E. Segal Oral History, 1991.
17. Amos Vogel Oral History, 1991.
18. Joanne Koch Oral History, 1992.
19. James R. Oestreich, "Inaugural Concert," *New York Times*, February 15, 1992.
20. Vincent Canby, *New York Times*, December 9, 1991.
21. Joanne Koch Oral History, 1992.
22. Joanne Koch, interview by Sharon Zane, January 2002.
23. Charles Wadsworth Oral History, 1990.

24. Ibid.
25. Miles Kastendieck, "Inaugural of Tully Hall Wins Exuberant Acclaim," *New York Post*, September 12, 1969.
26. Irving Kolodin, "Music to My Ears," *Saturday Review*, September 27, 1969.
27. Charles Wadsworth Oral History, 1990.
28. Edgar B. Young, *Lincoln Center: The Building of an Institution* (New York: New York University Press, 1980), p. 240.
29. Alice Tully Oral History, 1991.
30. Frank Taplin Oral History, 1993.
31. Bernard Holland, "Man Behind the Boom in Chamber Music," *Saturday Review*, September 1981.
32. Bernard Holland, "Wadsworth's Farewell to Chamber Society," *New York Times*, May 9, 1989.
33. Charles Wadsworth Oral History, 1990.
34. Bernard Holland, "Wadsworth's Farewell to Chamber Society," *New York Times*, May 9, 1989.
35. Allan Kozinn, *New York Times*, June 13, 1991.
36. Charles Wadsworth Oral History, 1990.
37. Peter Goodman, "New Chamber Music Society Director," *Newsday*, March 4, 1992.
38. Frank Taplin Oral History, 1993.
39. David Abrams, *Post-Standard* (Syracuse, N.Y.), January 30, 1998.
40. Susan Reiter, "Steps and Strings/Expanding Chamber Music with Bold New Dances," *Newsday*, January 29, 2002.
41. "New Chamber Music Directors for Lincoln Center," *Classics Today.com*, June 14, 2004.
42. Edgar B. Young, *Lincoln Center: The Building of an Institution* (New York: New York University Press, 1980), p. 88.
43. Robin Pogrebin, "A Drama Showcase at Middle Age Grapples with Identity," *New York Times*, August 23, 1999.
44. "Enter the Gadflies," *Newsweek*, February 8, 1965.
45. Mel Gussow, "Repertory Theater Battles Deficit Woes," *New York Times*, November 22, 1972.
46. Ibid.
47. *Newsweek*, February 1, 1971.
48. *The New Republic*, November 25, 1972.

49. *New York Times*, March 7, 1973.
50. Mel Gussow, "Costs Keep the Beaumont Dark, despite a Theater Booking Jam," *New York Times*, October 26, 1977.
51. Mel Gussow, "Beaumont Theater Will Reopen with 5-Member Directorate," *New York Times*, December 13, 1978.
52. Ibid.
53. "Redesign of Beaumont and State Theater Set with $8 Million Gift," by John Rockwell, *New York Times*, May 15, 1981.
54. Ibid.
55. Cyril Harris Oral History, 1990.
56. Letter from the Fan Fox and Leslie R. Samuels Foundation, Inc., to Lincoln Center for the Performing Arts, Inc., November 8, 1982, LCPA.
57. "A Historical Review by Dates of the Renovation Project," 1980–1983, the Vivian Beaumont Theater, Inc., among materials sent to Sharon Zane, along with a letter dated September 8, 2005, by Linda LeRoy Janklow, chairman emeritus, Lincoln Center Theater, Inc., LCPA.
58. Vivian Beaumont Theater Board of Directors Minutes Summary, December 6, 1982, among materials sent to Sharon Zane, along with a letter dated September 8, 2005, by Linda LeRoy Janklow, chairman emeritus, Lincoln Center Theater, Inc., LCPA.
59. Richmond Crinkley, "Beaumont Renovation," by Op Ed article, *New York Times*, October 18, 1983.
60. Harold Schonberg, *New York Times*, July 15, 1983.
61. Lincoln Center Board of Directors Minutes, August 24, 1983.
62. Martin E. Segal Oral History, 1991.
63. *Daily News*, November 18, 1983.
64. Dan Sullivan, *Los Angeles Times*, July 24, 1982.
65. Lincoln Center Board of Directors Minutes, June 4, 1984.
66. Leslie Bennetts, "Crinkley Out as Beaumont Director," *New York Times*, October 16, 1984.
67. Martin E. Segal Oral History, 1991.
68. Bernard Gersten Oral History, 1992.
69. Ibid.
70. Lincoln Center Board of Directors Minutes, March 21, 2005.
71. Ibid.
72. "School of American Ballet: History and Facts" (www.sab.org/background.htm).

73. Andrea Olmstead, *Juilliard: A History* (Chicago: University of Illinois Press, 1999), p. 211.
74. Lincoln Center Board of Directors Minutes, December 8, 1986.
75. "Agreement between Lincoln Center for the Performing Arts, Inc., and the School of American Ballet," Article III, May 4, 1987, LCPA.
76. Memorandum to Nathan Leventhal from Andre Mirabelli, October 31, 1986, LCPA.
77. "SAB Presents First Mae L. Wien Award and Becomes a Lincoln Center Constituent," Lincoln Center press release, May 4, 1987, LCPA.
78. Ibid.
79. Jennifer Dunning, "City Ballet's School Joins Lincoln Center," *New York Times*, May 5, 1987.
80. Nathan Leventhal Oral History, 2000.
81. "Positioning Lincoln Center to Meet the Challenges of the Future," Committee on the Future of Lincoln Center, Lincoln Center, Inc., May 1986, LCPA.
82. George Weissman Oral History, 1991–1992.
83. Robert Palmer, "Honoring the Classics of Jazz," *New York Times*, August 3, 1987.
84. Stuart Troup, "A Watershed 'Classical' Jazz Series," *Newsday*, August 2, 1987.
85. Lincoln Center, Inc., press release, June 16, 1963, LCPA.
86. Wynton Marsalis, "What Jazz Is—and Isn't," *New York Times*, July 31, 1988.
87. "Building a Jazz Constituent at Lincoln Center," Lincoln Center, Inc., 1990, LCPA.
88. H. Concurrent Resolution #57, passed by the U.S. House of Representatives, September 23, 1987; passed by the U.S. Senate, December 4, 1987, www.jazzai.org.
89. Gordon Davis Oral History, 1992.
90. "Building a Jazz Constituent at Lincoln Center," Lincoln Center, Inc., 1990, LCPA.
91. "Jazz in the Pantheon," *New York Times* editorial, January 13, 1991.
92. Lincoln Center Board of Directors Minutes, October 7, 1957.
93. "Creating a Jazz Constituent: A Progress Report," Lincoln Center, Inc., March 22, 1995, LCPA.
94. Wynton Marsalis, interview by Sharon Zane, 2002.

95. "Jazz at Lincoln Center Voted Lincoln Center Constituent," Lincoln Center, Inc., press release, December 18, 1995, LCPA.
96. Reynold Levy, interview by Stephen Stamas and Sharon Zane, December 20, 2004.
97. Gene Seymour, "Jazz Makes Grade at Lincoln Center," *Newsday*, December 19, 1995.
98. Nathan Leventhal Oral History, 2000.

Chapter 2. Filling Programming Gaps: Lincoln Center Presents

1. Press release, Lincoln Center, Inc., August 24, 1965, LCPA.
2. Ibid.
3. Carlos Moseley Oral History, 1991.
4. "Lockwood Keys Concert's Bills to Singer/Songwriter," *Billboard*, June 2, 1973.
5. Letter to Friends of Great Performers, Lincoln Center, Inc., April 1976, LCPA.
6. Lincoln Center Board of Directors Minutes, December 18, 1995.
7. Ibid.
8. "Report on Lincoln Center Programming Options," Lincoln Center, Inc., March 1996, LCPA.
9. Joseph Solman, ed., *Mozartiana* (New York: Walker & Company, 1990), p. 27.
10. "Report on Survey to Determine the Feasibility of Creating and Operating a Performing Arts Center in New York City," Day & Zimmerman, Engineers, 1955, LCPA.
11. Schuyler Chapin Oral History, 1991.
12. Lincoln Center Executive Committee Minutes, September 9, 1963.
13. Raymond Ericson, "Music: Mozart Series Is Off to an Excellent Start," *New York Times*, August 2, 1966.
14. Allan Kozinn, "Has Mostly Mozart Festival Worn Out Its Welcome?" *New York Times*, August 27, 1992.
15. "Basically Bill & Frankly Frederick," *Stagebill*, 1991.
16. Gerard Schwarz Oral History, 2001.
17. Ibid.
18. Ibid.
19. Ibid.
20. Allan Kozinn, "A Finale, Entirely, for Mozart and Schwarz," *New York Times*, August 27, 2001.

21. Martha Hostetter, "The Mostly Mozart Strike: Music, Money and Maybe Better Art," *Gotham Gazette*, September 1, 2002.
22. Peter G. Davis, "Moz Def," www.newyorkmetro.com, 2003.
23. "Avery Fisher Hall Reconfigured for Mostly Mozart Festival, Summer 2005," Lincoln Center, Inc., press release, May 3, 2005, LCPA.
24. Press release, Lincoln Center, Inc., June 10, 1966, LCPA.
25. Richard F. Shepard, "International All-Arts Festival Planned by Lincoln Center in '67," *New York Times*, June 15, 1966.
26. Lincoln Center Board of Directors Minutes, October 9, 1967.
27. Press release, Lincoln Center, Inc., February 26, 1968, LCPA.
28. Edgar B. Young, *Lincoln Center: The Building of an Institution* (New York: New York University Press, 1980), p. 297.
29. Lincoln Center Board of Directors Minutes, September 23, 1987.
30. Press release, Lincoln Center, Inc., May 19, 1987, LCPA.
31. Ibid.
32. David Sterritt, "Downtown Shows Please Uptown Hosts," *Christian Science Monitor*, August 11, 1987.
33. Lincoln Center Board of Directors Minutes, September 21, 1992.
34. John Rockwell, "Segal to Succeed Ames as Lincoln Center Chairman, *New York Times*, March 3, 1981.
35. "The New York International Festival of the Arts 1986–2001," December 2001, p. 6, LCPA.
36. Joseph C. Koenenn, "The NY Arts Festival: Was It a Success?" *Newsday*, July 12, 1988.
37. Allan Kozinn, "Has Mostly Mozart Festival Worn Out Its Welcome?" *New York Times*, August 27, 1992.
38. Jane Moss, "Lincoln Center Summer Programming Proposal," December 14, 1993, LCPA.
39. Lincoln Center Executive Committee Minutes, February 22, 1995.
40. Lincoln Center Festival press materials, prepared by the Kreisberg Group, for the 1996 Lincoln Center Festival, LCPA.
41. "Time Off: Diversions and Excursions July 16–29," *Wall Street Journal*, July 16, 1996.
42. Jeremy Gerard, "Cultural Revolution," *Variety*, August 19–26, 1996.
43. Lincoln Center Board of Directors Minutes, September 29, 1998.
44. "Report on Lincoln Center Programming Options," Lincoln Center, Inc., 1996, LCPA.

45. Nathan Leventhal Oral History, 2000.
46. Lincoln Center Executive Committee Minutes, April 25, 1996.
47. Deborah Grace-Winer, "Lincoln Center Creates a Home for American Pop," *New York Times*, January 31, 1999.
48. Fax transmission from Jonathan Schwartz, dated August 17, 1999, 2:05 P.M., LCPA.
49. Stephen Holden, "The Memory of Love's Refrain," *New York Times*, December 16, 1998.
50. Deborah Grace-Winer, "Lincoln Center Creates a Home for American Pop," *New York Times*, January 31, 1999.
51. Nathan Leventhal Oral History, 2000.
52. Lincoln Center Board of Directors Minutes, March 27, 2006.
53. John O'Keefe Oral History, 1992.
54. Ibid.
55. Letter from Robert N. Kreidler to Amyas Ames, October 24, 1975, Amyas Ames's scrapbook, LCPA.
56. Anthony Bliss Oral History, 1991.
57. Letter from Lincoln Kirstein to Amyas Ames, January 21, 1976, Amyas Ames's scrapbook, LCPA.
58. John Mazzola Oral History, 1991–1992.
59. Amyas Ames Oral History, 1990.
60. Leonard de Paur Oral History, 1990.
61. Ibid.
62. Edith Oliver, "The Theater (Off-Broadway)," *New Yorker*, September 4, 1971.
63. Jack Kroll, "Singing in the Sun," *Newsweek*, September 6, 1971.
64. Howard Thompson, "Street Theater Livens Lincoln Center," *New York Times*, August 20, 1971.
65. George Gent, "For City's Children, a Gift Waits at Lincoln Center," *New York Times*, December 8, 1971.
66. *Long Island Press*, December 23, 1971.
67. Carman Moore, "Soul at the Center," *Saturday Review*, August 26, 1972.
68. Lincoln Center Board of Directors Minutes, March 12, 1984.
69. Press release, Lincoln Center, Inc., June 17, 1974, LCPA.
70. Leonard de Paur obituary notice, *New York Times*, November 11, 1998.

71. Jenneth Webster, interview by Sharon Zane, April 2001.
72. Nathan Leventhal Oral History, 2000.
73. Press materials, Lincoln Center, Inc., November 17, 1987, and September 15, 1988, LCPA.
74. Meet-the-Artist promotional brochure, 1976, LCPA.
75. Letter from Barbara Stellman, the director of Meet-the-Artist, to Saller & Roskin, March 1, 1978, LCPA.
76. Press release, Lincoln Center, Inc., May 3, 1978, LCPA.
77. "Lincoln Center Loves Children," press release, Lincoln Center, Inc., October 15, 1996, LCPA.
78. Alina Bloomgarden Oral History, 2001.
79. The Celebration Series brochure, May 1985, LCPA.
80. Alina Bloomgarden Oral History, 2001, in which she reads the quoted material from a letter addressed to "To Whom It May Concern" and signed by Itzhak Perlman, LCPA.
81. Memorandum from Aline Bloomgarden to Nathan Leventhal, February 15, 1996, LCPA.
82. Mark Schubart, Vision Statement, "2001: 25th Anniversary," Lincoln Center Institute, LCPA.
83. Edgar B. Young, *Lincoln Center: The Building of an Institution* (New York: New York University Press, 1980), p. 232.
84. Charles Fowler, "Lincoln Center Institute: It Tangles with the Issues," *Musical America*, January 1982.
85. Paul Montgomery, "Lincoln Center Proposes Wider Youth Involvement," *New York Times*, April 17, 1972.
86. Mark Schubart Oral History, 1991–1992.
87. Paul Montgomery, "Lincoln Center Proposes Wider Youth Involvement," *New York Times*, April 17, 1972.
88. Ibid.
89. Lincoln Center Board of Directors Minutes, March 13, 1972.
90. Ibid.
91. Lincoln Center Board of Directors Minutes, May 20, 1974.
92. Ibid.
93. Lincoln Center Executive Committee Minutes, February 13, 1973.
94. June Dunbar Oral History, 1993.
95. Paul Montgomery, "Lincoln Center Proposes Wider Youth Involvement," *New York Times*, April 17, 1972.

96. June Dunbar Oral History, 1993.
97. Ibid.
98. Ibid.
99. Mark Schubart Oral History, 1991–1992.
100. June Dunbar Oral History, 1993.
101. Ibid.
102. "Executive Summary," Lincoln Center Institute Long-Range Plan, Lincoln Center Institute, 1996, LCPA.
103. Lincoln Center Board of Directors Minutes, March 28, 2000.
104. Scott Noppe-Brandon, interview by Susan DeMark, November 11, 2002.
105. Ibid.
106. "Lincoln Center Institute Launches New Education Excellence Competition," Lincoln Center Institute press release, May 4, 2006, LCPA.
107. John Kelly, "Adding Art to the Curriculum," *ParentGuide*, August 1995.

Chapter 3. The Changing Campus: Architecture and Art Serve the Community

1. Max Abramovitz Oral History, 1990.
2. Lincoln Center Board of Directors Minutes, December 1, 1980.
3. Agreement between the City of New York and Lincoln Center for the Performing Arts, Inc., for Re-Use Parcels #4c, 4d, Q-2a, Q-2b and 4b of the Lincoln Square Urban Renewal Area, February 1, 1966, LCPA.
4. Feasibility Study for Lincoln Center for the Performing Arts, Inc., of Proposed Combined-Use Building at 65th and 66th Streets and Amsterdam Avenue, New York City, Richard H. Koch, October 1980, Revised January 1981, LCPA.
5. Lincoln Center Board of Directors Minutes, December 12, 1983.
6. Ibid.
7. Martin E. Segal letter to Brendan Gill, August 20, 1991, LCPA.
8. Martin E. Segal Oral History, 1991.
9. Gordon J. Davis Oral History, 1992.
10. Lincoln Center Board of Directors Minutes, October 7, 1985.
11. Emily Torgan, "2nd Life for Lincoln Center Tower," *Westsider*, March 18–24, 1993.
12. George Weissman Oral History, 1991–1992.

13. Eleanor Blau, "Lincoln Center Seeking Funds for New Tower," *New York Times*, November 11, 1987.
14. Ibid.
15. Frederick P. Rose Oral History, 1991–1992.
16. Nathan Leventhal Oral History, 1991.
17. "The New Samuel B. & David Rose Building at Lincoln Center Opens," Lincoln Center, Inc., press release, November 19, 1990, LCPA.
18. Paul Goldberger, "A Shot of Cultural Adrenaline at Lincoln Center," *New York Times*, July 28, 1991.
19. Lewis Davis Oral History, 1995.
20. Ibid.
21. Nathan Leventhal Oral History, 1991.
22. George Weissman Oral History, 1991–1992.
23. Gordon Davis Oral History, 1992.
24. Martin E. Segal Oral History, 1991.
25. Herbert Kupferberg, "Lincoln Center Opens $19 Million Theater," *Herald Tribune*, April 24, 1964.
26. "Acoustics Scorned at State Theater," *New York Times*, May 20, 1964.
27. Philip Johnson Oral History, 1990.
28. Richard F. Shepard, "Schuman Discusses His Plans for Lincoln Center Harmony," *New York Times*, January 12, 1965.
29. Harold Schonberg, "New Acoustics for State Theater," *New York Times*, January 9, 1981.
30. Ibid.
31. Martin E. Segal letter to Mr. Leslie R. Samuels, July 19, 1982, LCPA.
32. Memorandum re: "Reconstruction of the State Theater and the Beaumont Theater," from Amyas Ames to Lincoln Center Executive Committee, May 14, 1981, LCPA.
33. Letter from John Mazzola to Henry Geldzahler, October 30, 1981, LCPA.
34. Philip Johnson Oral History, 1990.
35. Allan Kozinn, "Now It's City Opera's Turn to Fiddle with the Sound," *New York Times*, September 3, 1996.
36. Dinitia Smith, "Audience Reaction Is More Ho-Hum Than Outrage," *New York Times*, November 3, 1999.
37. Miriam Kreinin Souccar, "City Opera Eyes Trump Project, Other New Sites," *Crain's New York Business*, April 22–28, 2002.

38. Robin Pogrebin, "Opera Not a Shoo-In at Ground Zero," *New York Times*, June 30, 2003.
39. Ibid.
40. *New York Times*, November 15, 2004.
41. Edward Wyatt and Robin Pogrebin, "Trade Center Cultural Decisions Affected by What's Best for Lincoln Center," *New York Times*, June 15, 2004.
42. Ibid.
43. Donal Henahan, "Boulez and His Orchestra Express Pleasure at the New Sound of Music in Hall," *New York Times*, October 20, 1976.
44. Harold Schonberg, *New York Times*, October 20, 1976.
45. Ibid.
46. *New York Times*, October 27, 1976.
47. Andrew Porter, *New Yorker,* November 1, 1976.
48. Carlos Moseley Oral History, 1991.
49. *New York Times*, November 22, 1981.
50. Donal Henahan, *New York Times*, May 20, 1984.
51. Will Crutchfield, *New York Times*, September 28, 1987.
52. Memo from Avery Fisher to George Weissman, October 18, 1988, LCPA.
53. Memo from Nathan Leventhal to George Weissman, April 29, 1991, LCPA.
54. Letter from Nathan Leventhal to Stephen Stamas, August 13, 1991, New York Philharmonic Archives.
55. Letter from Stephen Stamas to Nathan Leventhal, August 27, 1991, LCPA.
56. At the press conference Kurt Masur was quoted as saying, "There is a kind of international rule that the ceiling over an orchestra should not be higher than a certain point." This led Cyril Harris to write to Nathan Leventhal objecting to Masur's statement. He pointed out that he had even been on record that while lowering the ceiling might help musicians to hear onstage, there would be an adverse effect on the acoustics in the hall. Letter from Cyril Harris to Nathan Leventhal, November 17, 1991, LCPA.
57. *New York Times*, November 16, 1991.
58. Peter Goodman, *Newsday*, September 19, 1992.

59. Joint statement by New York Philharmonic chairman Paul B. Guenther and Carnegie Hall chairman Sanford L. Weill, Monday, June 2, 2003, LCPA.
60. *New York Times*, October 8, 2003.
61. Ibid.
62. Bruce Crawford, interview by Stephen Stamas and Sharon Zane, December 20, 2004.
63. Thaddeus Crapster Oral History, 1997.
64. Edgar B. Young, *Lincoln Center: The Building of an Institution* (New York: New York University Press, 1980).
65. Vera List Oral History, 1994.
66. *The Advocate & Greenwich Time*, February 28, 1993.
67. Letter from Delmar Hendricks to Sharon Zane, May 2, 2002, LCPA.
68. Ibid.
69. Delmar Hendricks Oral History, 1997.
70. Thomas Lollar, interview by Sharon Zane, March 14, 2003.
71. "Lincoln Center Celebrates 30th Anniversary of Lincoln Center/List Poster and Print Program," Lincoln Center, Inc., press release #11993, LCPA.
72. Vera List Oral History, 1994.
73. Lincoln Center Executive Committee Minutes, March 25, 1982.
74. Martin E. Segal, interview by Sharon Zane, September 8, 2003.
75. Robin Duthy, "For the Love of Art," *Connoisseur*, May 1983.
76. Lincoln Center Arts & Acquisitions Committee Minutes, May 4, 1995, LCPA.
77. Lincoln Center Arts & Acquisitions Committee Minutes, November 18, 1997, LCPA.
78. Lincoln Center Board of Directors Minutes, December 18, 1998.
79. Lincoln Center Arts & Acquisitions Committee Minutes, February 14, 1996, LCPA.
80. Ibid.
81. "Debating a Sculpture with a Name and 4 Faces," *New York Times*, July 9, 1996.
82. Memorandum from Reynold Levy to the Lincoln Center Board of Directors and the Lincoln Center Directors Emeriti Council, July 14, 2004, LCPA.

Chapter 4. Making Things Happen: Leadership at Lincoln Center

1. Until March 1984, the by-laws of Lincoln Center made the chairman of the board the "senior officer of the Corporation" and the president, if any, the chief executive officer. In 1984, the president was designated the "chief operating officer," and the chairman remained "senior officer." (See Board of Directors Minutes, March 12, 1984.)
2. Addendum to Amyas Ames's Oral History, 1990: "A Concept of Lincoln Center, Inc.," by Amyas Ames, LCPA.
3. Ibid.
4. Edgar B. Young, *Lincoln Center: The Building of an Institution* (New York: New York University Press, 1980), p. 297.
5. Ibid.
6. Letter from C. Douglas Dillon to Amyas Ames, May 2, 1974, LCPA.
7. *New York Times*, April 8, 1970.
8. Lincoln Center Board of Directors Minutes, October 14, 1981.
9. Avery Fisher brochure, Lincoln Center for the Performing Arts, 2000, LCPA.
10. Addendum to Amyas Ames's Oral History, 1990: "A Concept of Lincoln Center, Inc.," by Amyas Ames.
11. John Rockwell, "Segal to Succeed Ames as Lincoln Center Chairman," *New York Times*, March 3, 1981.
12. Ibid.
13. "Mazzola Offers Reason for His Resignation," *New York Times*, September 17, 1982.
14. Samuel G. Freedman, "Lincoln Center Chief Is Resigning," *New York Times*, December 2, 1983.
15. "Positioning Lincoln Center to Meet the Challenges of the Future," Committee on the Future, May 1986, LCPA.
16. Ibid.
17. Ibid.
18. Ibid.
19. Letter from Martin E. Segal to Charter Associates, December 14, 1981, LCPA.
20. "New Martin E. Segal Award for Young Performers Is Announced," Lincoln Center, Inc., press release, June 23, 1986, LCPA.
21. Edgar Young, *Lincoln Center: The Building of an Institution* (New York: New York University Press, 1980), p. 106.

22. George Weissman Oral History, 1991–1992.
23. William F. May Oral History, 1995.
24. George Weissman Oral History, 1991–1992.
25. Ibid.
26. Ibid.
27. Ibid.
28. Lincoln Center Board of Directors Minutes, June 13, 1994.
29. Memorandum from Nathan Leventhal to Lincoln Center Staff, January 24, 1994, LCPA.
30. Allan Kozinn, "Beverly Sills Is Named by Unanimous Vote to Head Lincoln Center," *New York Times*, January 25, 1994.
31. Kathy Larkin, "Taking Over Lincoln Center," *Hackensack Daily Record*, February 1, 1994.
32. Ralph Blumenthal, "Beverly Sills, at 66, Stars in Her Grandest Role," *New York Times*, February 13, 1996.
33. Ibid.
34. Ralph Blumenthal, "Beverly Sills Names Date of Resignation," *New York Times*, April 2, 2002.
35. Ibid.
36. Letter from Gordon J. Davis to Beverly Sills, September 27, 2001, LCPA.
37. *Los Angeles Times*, September 29, 2001.
38. "Frank A. Bennack, Jr. Nominated to Succeed Bruce Crawford as Chairman, Lincoln Center Board, Effective June, 2005," Lincoln Center press release, May 5, 2005, LCPA.
39. Frank A. Bennack Jr., interview by Sharon Zane, June 26, 2006.
40. Reynold Levy, interview by Sharon Zane, June 26, 2006.
41. Frank A. Bennack Jr., interview by Sharon Zane, June 26, 2006.
42. Ibid.

Chapter 5. A New Look: Redevelopment and Renewal

1. John W. Mazzola Memorandum to Files, October 15, 1981, LCPA.
2. Lincoln Center Board of Directors Minutes, March 30, 1998.
3. Ibid.
4. Lincoln Center Board of Directors Minutes, December 6, 1999.
5. Justin Davidson, "Costly Upgrade Seen for Center," *Newsday*, December 8, 1999.
6. Ralph Blumenthal, "Met Opera Rejects Plan for Renovation of Lincoln Center," *New York Times*, January 24, 2001.

7. Ibid.
8. Lincoln Center Executive Committee Minutes, February 15, 2001.
9. Robin Pogrebin, "Met Is Rejoining the Project to Renovate Lincoln Center," *New York Times*, May 4, 2001.
10. Lincoln Center Board of Directors Minutes, October 1, 2001.
11. Robin Pogrebin, "Chairman of Lincoln Center Redevelopment Resigns," *New York Times*, October 11, 2001.
12. "2nd Departure at Lincoln Center," *Newsday*, January 3, 2002.
13. Lincoln Center Board of Directors Minutes, March 26, 2002.
14. Robin Pogrebin, "Reining In Expectations on Lincoln Center Project," *New York Times*, July 9, 2002.
15. Lincoln Center Board of Directors Minutes, January 23, 2003.
16. "Innovative Architecture Team Selected to Redesign Lincoln Center Public Spaces," Lincoln Center, Inc., press release, February 24, 2003, LCPA.
17. Robin Pogrebin, "Lincoln Center Proceeds Modestly," *New York Times*, May 8, 2003.
18. Robin Pogrebin, "Lincoln Center Redevelopment Chairman Has Resigned," *New York Times*, June 13, 2003.
19. "Lincoln Center Unveils Dynamic Diller Scofidio + Renfro Design for West 65th Street," Lincoln Center, Inc., press release, April 13, 2004, LCPA.
20. Herbert Muschamp, "You Say You Want an Evolution? O.K., Then Tweak," *New York Times*, April 13, 2004.
21. Justin Davidson, "Lightness of Being," *Newsday*, April 14, 2004.
22. Reynold Levy, interview by Sharon Zane, June 26, 2006.
23. Lincoln Center Executive Committee Minutes, January 5, 2005.
24. Lincoln Center Board of Directors Minutes, March 21, 2005.
25. Ibid.
26. "Transforming Lincoln Center," *Inside Lincoln Center*, Lincoln Center, Inc., Spring 2006, LCPA.
27. Reynold Levy, interview by Stephen Stamas and Sharon Zane, December 20, 2004.
28. Bruce Crawford, interview by Stephen Stamas and Sharon Zane, December 20, 2004.
29. Reynold Levy, interview by Sharon Zane, June 26, 2006.

CREDITS

Sandor Acs, pages 120 and 167
Bill Anderson, page 125
Bachrach, page 154 (bottom)
Stephanie Berger, pages 74, 75, and 95
Michael C. Burke, page 154 (top)
Peter Bussian, page 175
CBS Photo, page128
Diller Scofidio + Renfro, pages 191, 192, 193, and 198
Peter Duffin, page 173
Ken Friedman, page 62
Great Ji, page 71
Steven Haas, page 5
Chester Higgins, Jr., page 172
Paul Hosefros/*New York Times*, page 3
Paul Jeremias, page 60
Keith Major, page 48
Jack Manning/*New York Times*, page 89
Julie Maris/Semel, page 139
Carl Mydans, page 10
Alane Poirier, page 94

Bob Serating, page 134
Julie Skarratt, page 49
Susanne Faulkner Stevens, pages 18, 21, 32, 44, 53, 54, 68, 79, 85, 86, 91, 93, 99, 104, 113, and 148
Richard Termine, pages 56 and 197
Jack Vartoogian, pages 64 and 77
Ruby Washington/*New York Times*, page 34
Laine Wilser, page 39

INDEX

Page numbers in *italic* type refer to illustrations.